The Art of Letter Writing

The New Guide
to Writing More Effective Letters
for All Occasions

By Lassor A. Blumenthal

A PERIGEE BOOK

To Martha, with love

Perigee Books
are published by
The Putnam Publishing Group
200 Madison Avenue
New York, NY 10016

Published simultaneously in Canada by
General Publishing Co. Limited, Toronto
Second Perigee printing, 1985

Library of Congress Cataloging-in-Publication Data

Blumenthal, Lassor A.
  The art of letter writing.

  Reprint. Originally published: Grosset & Dunlap, 1977.
  Includes index.
  1. Letter-writing.   2. English language—
Rhetoric.   I. Title.
PE1485.B55 1985   395'.4   85-6328
ISBN 0-399-51174-1

Printed in the United States of America

    5   6   7   8   9   10

Contents

1. It's Easy to Write a Good Letter

You WILL FIND it easy to write effective letters if you practice the simple suggestions outlined in this book.

In these pages, we'll be discussing the three kinds of letters you'll be most likely to write:

1. *Formal letters, such as formal invitations to weddings.* These letters usually have a standard wording. This book gives you models for most of them; all you have to do is adapt the form to your needs.

2. *Informal letters to friends and relatives.* Such letters are usually substitutes for face-to-face conversations. Throughout this book, you'll find suggestions for writing good letters of this kind.

3. *Special-purpose letters.* These are written to achieve a goal. Typical are the letters you write to a company to ask for information, and to a department store to explain that in spite of what the computer says, you can't possibly owe $3,000,000.

EIGHT WAYS TO A GOOD LETTER

Here are eight suggestions for writing effective letters quickly and easily.

1. *Assemble your writing tools.* Get plenty of scratch paper and a pen or several pencils. And give yourself a comfortable working surface.

Scratch paper is necessary so that you can freely try out different ideas and words and cross out the ones you don't like.

In drafting a letter, I use a pencil because I like to erase rather than cross out. The pencil must have a sharp point because it makes me feel more efficient, and it seems to keep the ideas flowing.

2. *Decide on the main subject you're going to devote your letter to, and resolve to write only about that.* If you write about several subjects instead of concentrating on one, the reader won't know where to focus and the impact of your letter will decrease.

For example, when you write to your senator, you may want to talk about high taxes, crooked politicians, and the poor condition of the city transit system. If you select just one of those topics and write your whole letter about it, your senator will think that's what's really important to you, and will pay attention to it.

Another example: A store notifies you that your unpaid bill is three months overdue, and that it's going to turn the bill over to its lawyers. The fact is, you haven't paid the bill because you returned the merchandise. Your letter will explain this. At the same time, you're angry with the store because one of its clerks has been very rude. I suggest that you send two letters, in two different envelopes. In one letter, explain why you haven't paid the bill. In the other letter, complain about the clerk.

Why do it this way? Because the billing letter will go to the credit department, where someone can take care of it, and the letter of complaint will go to the personnel department, where a different person will, presumably, take care of the wretched clerk.

If you send one letter covering both problems, it will go to either the credit department or the personnel department, and will lie there in someone's folder until the problem under that department's jurisdiction is cleared up. Then—if you are lucky—it will be sent by interoffice mail to the other department. If you aren't lucky, it will be filed away or thrown away.

In settling on your one idea, it may be useful to jot down on a sheet of scratch paper just what it is, for example:

I want them to explain my Medicaid status.
I want them to send me information about their products.
I want to tell them about the kind of house I want to buy.

Put that sheet aside where you can glance at it as you write the letter, so that it will serve as a reminder to stick to your subject.

3. *Beginning a letter is usually the hardest part. Write down the single most important idea you want your reader to know. This idea will become the first sentence of your letter.*

After you've written your first thought on a scratch sheet, ask yourself: Is that really the most important thing I want to say? If it isn't, cross it out and start again.

Here are a couple of examples.

My landlord forgot to connect my apartment to a new intercom system in our building. After four months and many useless phone calls, I was really angry. I wrote:

Dear Mr. Smith:
I'm outraged at the way you've treated me during the past four months about the intercom.

When I thought about it, I realized that he already knew I was outraged, and it had, so far, made no difference. The most important thing I wanted to tell him was that *if he didn't connect my apartment I wasn't going to pay any more rent.* So I wrote:

Dear Mr. Smith:
I plan to withhold future rent payments until you install my intercom.

This opening sentence was clear and simple, and it led naturally to the rest of the letter.

Another example: I decided to write to my local newspaper about a budget matter concerning our town's sanitation department. My first effort went like this:

Dear Editor:
It isn't often that I write to the editor to express my opinion.

When I thought about it, I realized that no one cares how often I write. So I rewrote the opening:

Dear Editor:
I believe we should give the Sanitation Department the money it's requested for a new garage.

That version left no doubt about why I was writing.

To repeat the general rule: Your first sentence should be about the most important thing you want your reader to know.

4. *Immediately explain or clarify your first sentence.* Write down whatever comes into your head, no matter how half-baked or unclear it may seem.

Many people are afraid to write the first words they think of. They feel they're committing themselves forever, or that the words in their heads aren't exactly what they want to say. So they juggle words and ideas in their minds until finally, as with any juggling act that goes on too long, the whole thing comes crashing down in a hopeless jumble.

Save yourself that agony. Write down *all* the thoughts that come into your head. Once they're on paper, you can see what you like or dislike about them, and you can change them as you want.

Let's illustrate this proposition with the letters we've started. After I had settled on the first sentence of my landlord letter—"I plan to withhold future rent payments until you install my intercom"—I wrote:

> My patience is at an end. You never do anything you promise. This has been a tremendous inconvenience to me and my family, and I won't put up with it any longer.

When I looked it over, I realized that the paragraph was a little like a garbage pail. I was dumping everything into it.

So, following the rule of "Explain or clarify your first sentence," my final draft said:

> I plan to withhold future rent payments until my intercom is installed.
> I am doing this because you have left me with no intercom for four months. As you know, I have spoken to you or your agents at least eight times. In spite of promises and excuses, my intercom is still unconnected.

The second paragraph explains the reason behind the opening sentence.

As another example, consider the letter to the editor that I mentioned earlier, which began: "I believe we should give the Sanitation Department the money it's requested for a new garage." The second paragraph explained why:

> More than half of the present equipment now has to stay outside because there's no room to store it. This causes the machines to deteriorate faster, so we need to replace them sooner. If we fail to build a new garage now, it will cost us more later.

Notice that the second paragraph explains the reasons behind the first statement.

To repeat: As a general rule, the second paragraph should explain or clarify the first.

5. *Suggest some action.* End your letter by mentioning some action that you plan to take or that you'd like the reader to take.

For example, my letter to the landlord ended with this paragraph:

> As soon as you connect my intercom, I'll be happy to send you my rent.

The letter about the Sanitation Department ended:

Any citizen concerned about saving money should vote in favor of appropriating money for the new garage.

In both endings, the readers were urged to take some kind of action.

6. *Put the letter away for at least a couple of hours. Then reread it.*
Frequently, we get so involved in our writing that we think it's clearer than it is. A good way to make sure that a letter is clear is to come back to it fresh. Putting it away for a couple of hours is one way to do this. Putting it away overnight is even better.

When you do read the letter again, it will be almost new to you, and you'll have a better idea of whether the recipient will get the message you want to deliver.

7. *Eliminate ruthlessly.* Nobody has enough time—for anything. This is especially true of letter readers. The longer the letter, the less likely the reader will go through it. So, to make sure that what you write is read, eliminate every sentence, every phrase, every word not needed.

As a general rule, the shorter your letter, the better. If you can keep it under a page, do so.

8. *Ask for criticism.* Ask someone whose opinion you respect to read the letter and criticize it. While this step isn't always necessary or possible, I've often found it useful in improving longer or more important letters.

Usually I ask my wife what she thinks. Sometimes I don't agree with her, and therefore I don't make the changes she recommends. But just as frequently she points out words that might be improved, or certain ideas that might be changed to make the letter sharper and clearer.

So, if you have someone whose opinion you value, you may find his or her opinion quite useful.

If you follow these eight suggestions, you'll find it easy to write a good letter. Of course, there are other things to think about. You'll want to avoid misspelled words, clichés, and poor grammar. (You'll find useful hints about these in Chapter 17.) And you'll want the letter to look good on paper. (That's discussed in Chapter 20.) But the eight ideas in this chapter will help you to construct a clear, readable letter which the recipient will understand and react to.

Good luck, and good writing!

2. Invitations to Everything

INVITATIONS ARE AS varied as the people who send them and the reasons for which they're sent. But basically they can be divided into two broad groups: informal and formal. The groups aren't always distinct: some invitations are a little bit of both.

In this chapter, you'll find many examples of all kinds of invitations. But whether you decide to copy one of these or to make up your own, make sure that you include the following information:

Reason for the invitation. Is it a birthday, an anniversary, or just for fun?

Date of the affair. Preferably both the date and the day of the week; that is, "Tuesday, June 17."

Time the affair starts. And, if you want, the time it will end. This is a courtesy to your guests: it lets them plan the rest of their day after the party. For example: "The luncheon will be from 12:30 to 2:00."

Location of the affair. Include the name of the building, if it has one, and the street address. If the affair is being held in a hotel or a building with a number of meeting rooms, give the room name or number: "In the Grand Ballroom of the Hotel Sumerset, 45 Boylston Street, Brooklyn."

You may also want to consider putting in the following information:

R.S.V.P.: These initials at the bottom of your invitation mean "Please let me know whether you're coming to the affair." They stand for *"Répondez, s'il vous plait"*—French for "Please answer."

What kind of clothes to wear. If dress is optional, you may want to say so; if guests are expected to wear a particular kind of outfit, that should be mentioned.

INFORMAL INVITATIONS

Party

For an informal party, you may want to send a short personal letter or a note.

The following letter assumes that the recipient knows the writer's address. Of course, it may be written on stationery that has the writer's address printed out.

> Dear Ella:
> We're having a party at our house for Bill's 50th birthday.
> It will be on Saturday, August 12, from 2:30 to 5:00. Bring your swim suit and enjoy the new pool.
> We are looking forward to seeing you.

New Year's Eve Party

Here's an enthusiastic letter. It makes the party sound like fun, and the writer's house the place to be on New Year's Eve. Enthusiasm is always a good thing to aim for in an informal party invitation.

Dear Jim:
We're having a stupendous party at our house to welcome the New Year. It begins at about 8:00 on December 31, and ends . . . who knows when. If you and Martha can come, it will make it even more stupendous. Please make it.

Dinner

It's courteous to mention that there will be other guests when you send a dinner invitation.

Dear Mr. and Mrs. Harrison:
Can you come for dinner on Monday night, January 13th, at eight o'clock? We're having two other couples whom I think you'll enjoy meeting.

Sincerely,

Children's Party

As this example shows, a children's party invitation is basically the same as an adult's.

Dear Tom:
I'm having a birthday party on Saturday afternoon, August 12th, at my house, starting at 2:00.
I hope you'll be able to come.

Mary

Special Event

Whatever the special event, use the checklist on page 9 to make sure you've covered the essential points.

Dear Aunt Mary:
Joan is taking her First Communion on Sunday, April 4, at the First Calvary Church in Huntington Square. Services will start at 9:00.
Joan, Jim, and I hope that you'll be able to come, and that afterwards you'll visit us for a buffet luncheon for a few close friends and relatives.
Please come; it's time we enjoyed the pleasure of your company again.

Love,

Christening

The important thing in any personal invitation is to give the facts and make the letter warm and simple.

Dear Aunt Harriet:
James Michael will be christened at Holy Name Church, 14th Street and Avenue D, Sunday, March 2, at two o'clock. After the ceremony, we hope you can come to a small gathering at our house.

Love,

Dear Joe:
    We're having a Berith for our son, Adam, on Thursday, July 14th, at 1:00, at Central Hospital.
    Marge and I will be very happy if you can come.
                                                    Love,

Commercial and Noncommercial Invitational Cards

You may want to send cards rather than a letter, especially if you're inviting many people. It's in perfectly good taste to use the commercial cards that have spaces for you to fill in the time and place of the party.

If you prefer, however, you can make up your own. Whether you use plain card-size paper—about four inches by six inches—or a larger sheet is a matter of personal preference. If you're not confident of your taste, your best bet is to be conservative: use a commercial card, or buy plain notepaper at a stationery store and make up your own message.

FORMAL INVITATIONS

Formal invitations may be divided into two kinds: handwritten and printed. The wording is usually the same in both. If you plan to do a lot of entertaining, you may want to have cards printed or engraved, with space for you to fill in the details.

Here's a standard style, with the handwritten parts not filled in:

Mr. and Mrs. Harrison Cobler
request the pleasure of

company at_____
on_____
at_____o'clock_____
10 Bristow Drive

You can do the whole thing by hand, if you prefer. It will look like this:

Mr. and Mrs. Harrison Cobler
request the pleasure of
Mr. and Mrs. Carl Samovar's
company at dinner
on December 25th
at eight o'clock
10 Bristow Drive

FORMAL WEDDING INVITATIONS

If you're having a very formal wedding, you'll want a very formal wedding invitation. (If it's a very informal wedding, of course, the invitation should be informal.)

For formal invitations, you'll visit a local printer or stationery store, or the stationery counter of a department store. They'll have a variety of sample books from which you can choose your invitations.

Two styles of lettering will be available: *Script* and roman are equally suitable.

Normally, formal wedding invitations are enclosed within two envelopes. The outer envelope is addressed in the standard way, to "Mr.," or "Mrs.," or "Ms.," or a combination such as "Mr. and Mrs." Your name and return address go on the upper left-hand corner.

The inner envelope (which, incidentally, has no glue) is addressed to the people you're inviting to the wedding. Use only their last names:

Mr. and Mrs. Merriway

If you're inviting other members of the family, too, add their names:

Mr. and Mrs. Merriway
Miss Helen Merriway
Mr. Joseph Bridgewater

If the invitee is a close friend or relative, the bride may write more informally on the inner envelope:

Uncle Jim and Aunt Melissa
Bill and Mary

Previously Unmarried Woman

The usual formal wedding invitation reads:

Mrs. and Mrs. George Granger
request the honor of your presence
at the marriage of their daughter
Martha Ann Granger
to
William James Jackson
on Sunday, the twenty-second of January
at four o'clock
Union Baptist Church
Smithtown

If the bride's mother has remarried, the invitation might read:

Mr. and Mrs. Milton Hightower
request the honor of your presence
at the marriage of Mrs. Hightower's daughter
Martha Ann Granger
etc.

Or, the invitation might be worded this way:

Mrs. Milton Hightower
and
Mr. George Granger
request the honor of your presence
at the marriage of their daughter
Martha Ann Granger
etc.

Widow

The invitation for a widow is the same as that for a previously unmarried woman, except that the bride's married name is used:

Mr. and Mrs. John Cruikshank
request the honor of your presence
at the marriage of their daughter
Geraldine Cruikshank Dodge
to
Dr. Frederick Wisdom

Divorcée

The invitation for a divorcée is the same as that for a previously unmarried woman, except that . . .

Mr. and Mrs. John Cruikshank
request the honor of your presence
at the marriage of their daughter
Jennifer Cruikshank Dodge
to
Mr. Gordon A. Roberts

Sent by Someone Other Than the Parents

When grandparents, uncles, or aunts issue the wedding invitation, the wording is changed accordingly:

Mr. and Mrs. George Rivlin
request the honor of your presence
at the marriage of their granddaughter [or niece]
Susan Morse
etc.

When the sender of the invitation is a friend, but not related, the wording is:

Mr. Benjamin Maure
requests the honor of your presence
at the marriage of
Lelia Mae Cranston
etc.

If the bride is sending the invitation herself, it reads:

> The honor of your presence
> is requested at the marriage of
> Miss Rona Winstead
> etc.

When Bride or Groom Is in the Service

When the bride or groom is in military service, the invitations are identical with those described above, except that it's customary to identify the service connection.

If the bride is in the service, the invitation will read:

> marriage of their daughter
> Phyllis Johnson
> Ensign, Nurse Corps, United States Navy

If the groom is in service, the invitation will read:

> to
> Phillip Johnson
> Captain, United States Army

If the groom is a noncommissioned officer or an enlisted man, the military designation may be included or omitted.

> James Audubon
> Yeoman, 1st Class, U.S. Navy

At-Home Cards

You can enclose at-home cards in the wedding invitations to let people know when you'll be ready for visitors. These cards are usually plain white and measure about two and three-quarters by four inches. Two typical forms are:

> Mr. and Mrs. Melvin Prebble
> After the third of January
> 14 Crescent Lane, Briarcliff

> At Home
> After January third
> 14 Crescent Lane
> Briarcliff

Receptions

You may want to invite all the wedding guests to a reception after the wedding. Use this form:

Mr. and Mrs. Garson Greyson
request the honor of your presence
at the marriage of their daughter
Gilda Grant
to
Mr. Glen Garibaldi
on Friday, the twelfth of June
at half after four o'clock
Community Church
and afterward at the reception
West End Country Club

R.s.v.p.

If you're inviting some guests to the reception whom you're not inviting to the wedding, here's the preferred wording:

Mrs. Margaret Pullett
requests the pleasure of your company
at the wedding reception of her daughter
Thyrsis Devon
and
Mr. Peter Paul Mound
on Saturday, the 13th of August
at two o'clock
Arbordale Plaza
The Bronx

R.s.v.p.

And if you're inviting some guests to the wedding but not to the reception, you'll want a special card to insert into the wedding invitations of those whom you're inviting to the reception. The card can be about three by four inches, in the same paper stock as the wedding invitation.

Mr. and Mrs. Harvey Banker
request the pleasure of your company
on Sunday, the third of April
at six o'clock
Mama Quintero's Restaurant
29 Balmoral Avenue
Nantasket

R.s.v.p.

INFORMAL WEDDING INVITATIONS

Informal weddings call for informal invitations. Keep them short, informative, and friendly.

Dear Howard:
   Our daughter, Elaine, will be married to Jack Boyle on Saturday, March 14, at three P.M. in an informal ceremony at our house.
   We hope you can come, and can stay after the ceremony for a small party.
                                        Cordially,

WEDDING POSTPONEMENTS AND CANCELLATIONS

If you have to cancel or postpone a wedding you've announced formally, the following three models will cover virtually any situation:

Mrs. Morgan Stanley
regrets exceedingly
that owing to the recent death of
Mr. Morgan Stanley
the invitations to the marriage of their daughter
Rachael May
to Mr. Richard Roebuck
must be recalled

Mr. and Mrs. Morgan Stanley
announce that the marriage of their daughter
Rachael May
to Mr. Richard Roebuck
will not take place

Mr. and Mrs. Morgan Stanley
announce that the marriage of their daughter
Rachael May
to Mr. Richard Roebuck
has been postponed from
Saturday, the first of November,
until
Friday, the fifteenth of December,
at two o'clock
Church of All Souls
Cambridge

ANNIVERSARY INVITATIONS

Formal

Most printers and stationers can supply model wording for formal, engraved anniversary invitations. A typical format is this one:

John Broadbent and Martha Broadbent Ames,
the children of
Jim and Ellen Broadbent,
cordially invite you to a dinner
celebrating their parents'
Golden Wedding Anniversary
Saturday November 9th
at eight o'clock
Wappinger's Restaurant
42 Carmine Street
Methuen

R.s.v.p.   Formal Dress

Informal

Dear Aunt Mary:

We're going to celebrate my parents' Golden Wedding anniversary with a dinner at eight o'clock, on Saturday, November 9th. It will be held at Wappinger's Restaurant, 42 Carmine Street, Methuen. Dress will be informal.

Please let me know if you'll be able to celebrate with us; we do hope you can come.

Fondly,

INVITATIONS TO VISIT

In extending a written invitation to visit, make sure that you tell your prospective guests: (1) when you'd like them to come; (2) how long you expect them to stay; (3) whether they should bring along any special items; (4) whether anyone else will be visiting at the same time.

Dear Barbara:

Jerry and I would love to have you visit us during your Christmas vacation. How about staying for a week, say from December 23rd to January 1st?

My brother, Hank, will be in town then, and is also staying with us.

As you know, the skiing and skating are usually terrific here at that time, so bring your equipment if you want; you can also rent skis and skates locally.

Let us know if you can come, and we'll make arrangements to pick you up.

Please say yes, and make us all very happy.

Fondly,

3. Answering Invitations

WHEN ANSWERING INVITATIONS, observe these common-sense rules:

1. Be gracious, whether you accept or refuse.
2. If you accept, confirm the major items in the invitation, that is, the time, place, etc.
3. Follow the style of the invitation: if it's a formal invitation, give a formal answer; if it's an informal invitation, make an informal reply. Generally, it gives a warmer impression if you answer in your own handwriting. This is true of formal as well as informal invitations.

INFORMAL REPLIES

Acceptances

Informal acceptances should be brief and warm. Address the letter to the signer of the invitation. If two people sign it, send your response to both.

> Dear Jan and Mel:
> Bill and I will be delighted to come to your 20th Anniversary party, on January 12th.
> We're looking forward to seeing you then, at eight o'clock.
>
> Cordially,

While it's not absolutely necessary to mention the time and place, it reassures the host that you have the right information.

> Dear Harry:
> Thanks so much for inviting us to your New Year's Eve affair.
> We wouldn't miss it for anything.
> We'll see you at the Harbin Inn at 8:00 for dinner.
>
> Best wishes,

Informal responses can be as enthusiastic or as merry as the occasion warrants.

> Dear Joanna:
> I think it's great that you're having a shower for Marianne. And of course I'll be delighted to come and see all of you again.
> Just to confirm the time and place: three o'clock, Saturday, June 27. See you then.
>
> Marge

Youngster's Acceptance

A youngster's response to an invitation should be simple. Anything elaborate looks artificial.

> Dear Ellen:
> Thanks for inviting me to your birthday party on Saturday afternoon, February 2nd.
> It will be very nice seeing you then.

Refusals

The main point about refusals is to make them sincere, and to show that you're sorry you can't come.

> Dear Bob:
> We're sorry that we'll be out of town on the day of your party. We'll have to make up for it with a get-together for just the four of us sometime soon.
> Have a wonderful time—and we'll be thinking of you.

When you write your letter, think about how the recipient will feel. If your absence will be a big disappointment, perhaps you can suggest another meeting.

> Dear Mr. Anderson:
> Because of a previous engagement, I won't be able to accept your dinner invitation for Friday evening, April 13th.
> As you might guess, I'm quite sorry about not being able to attend. I promise to visit you before long and bring you up to date on my travels.
> Cordially,

If you have to refuse an old friend, express your particular disappointment.

> Dear Howard:
> Why must you have your anniversary affair on the very day we'll be en route to Holland?
> I don't imagine you can transfer the party to Amsterdam, can you?
> We'll miss seeing you and the family and all our friends. But we'll make up for it with a long visit when we get back from Europe.
> In the meantime, you know that our very warmest wishes go to you and Elaine on this loveliest of occasions.
> Fondly,

FORMAL REPLIES

Responses to formal invitations should be in kind. A formal invitation to dinner, like that on page 11, can be answered:

> Mr. and Mrs. Carl Samovar
> accept with pleasure
> Mr. and Mrs. Cobler's
> kind invitation for dinner
> on December 25th
> at eight o'clock

If only one of you can go, the acceptance will read:

Mrs. Carl Samovar
accepts with pleasure
Mr. and Mrs. Cobler's
kind invitation for dinner
on December 25th
at eight o'clock
but regrets that
Mr. Samovar
will be absent at that time

If neither of you can attend, the response will read:

Mr. and Mrs. Carl Samovar
regret that they are unable to accept
Mr. and Mrs. Cobler's
kind invitation for December 25th.

The same general format is followed for all formal responses. Thus, for a wedding invitation like that on page 15, the proper response of the invitee is:

Mrs. John Nason
accepts with pleasure
the kind invitation of
Mr. and Mrs. Greyson
to the marriage of their daughter
Gilda Grant
to
Mr. Glen Garibaldi
on Friday, the twelfth of June
at half after four o'clock
Community Church
and afterward at
West End Country Club

If you have to refuse, simply substitute, as follows:

Mrs. John Nason
regrets that she is unable to accept
the kind invitation of
etc.

4. Social Letters to Friends and Relations

Do you find it difficult to write interesting, newsy letters? Do you feel that nothing exciting ever happens to you—at least, nothing that you can put in a letter? If you do, here are some suggestions that will help you to put together letters that others will want to read, and that will make them think you have an interesting life.

1. *If you have trouble getting started, forget about starting: just jump into the middle.* That is, talk about whatever is most important to you. Once you're finished, you may find that the middle was where you really wanted to begin anyway.

2. *If you can't think of where to jump in, use the following list of topics as memory joggers:*

Things you might discuss about yourself:
- What's made you laugh recently?
- Have you seen any plays, movies, or other entertainments you want to tell your correspondent about?
- What scandal is making tongues wag on your block, in your neighborhood, your community?
- Has anything exciting or unusual happened to any relatives or friends recently—especially your parents or your children?
- What changes are taking place in your community that you think are important or good or bad?
- Have you bought anything for yourself or any friends or family members?
- Are you planning on doing anything new or unusual? How about friends or relatives: do they plan to do anything new or unusual that your correspondent would want to know about?
- What do you think about the President? What do you think about your mayor? Have they done anything unusually brilliant or crooked or silly lately?

3. *Think about the person you're writing to: what is he or she interested in that you might write about?* For example: Has he or she any hobbies or other interests that you can comment on? For instance, if your correspondent collects stamps, he or she would undoubtedly be interested in knowing about a stamp exhibition in your town. Similarly, if he or she is a sports fan or interested in gourmet cooking—what connection can you make?

4. *As a general rule, talk about pleasant things rather than unpleasant.* "Laugh and the world laughs with you, cry and you cry alone" is as true in correspondence as it is in face-to-face relationships.

Here's a letter from an older person living in a retirement home where very little happens from day to day. Nevertheless, she makes it interesting:

Dear Folks:

All is quiet on the Centerville front.

I've kept healthy, thank goodness. And I've adjusted to staying here—pretty well!

There's quite a bit of ice on the ground now, so we don't get out as much as usual. But the icicles hanging outside my window are beautiful to look at, especially when the sun comes through them.

The food is improving—both in quantity and quality. A special treat last night: chocolate chip cookies: my favorites. Mmmm!

My great-nephew, Bill, and his wife came to visit last Saturday. It's been two years since I've seen him, so he was a sight for sore eyes.

Good friends are such a comfort; that's why I'm grateful I have you two.

Stay well, and go well.

Lovingly,

Young people frequently find it difficult to write to older people because they often seem to have so little in common with them. If you're in this position, remember that everyone enjoys funny stories or an incident that will bring a smile. You may be able to build your letter around one:

Dear Aunt Mary:

School has been pretty much of a grind recently, but I did want to thank you for the socks you sent. I now have the proudest feet on campus.

Did you see the story in your paper about our local heroine?

There is a poor woman here who inherited $200,000 from her father's estate. She went through the whole thing in a few months. She told a local reporter: "We bought cars and motorcycles for the boys and a truck and a $2000 hi-fi, and clothes, and we put a down payment on a house and the girls and I had all our teeth capped and I had my breasts lifted, and we all saw a psychiatrist and we spent $5000 on new furniture .... Then all of a sudden we realized we were broke."

When they asked her if she was sorry, she said, "Yes, but if I had the chance again, I'd do exactly the same thing I did—blow it!"

So, even though this is a small town, we have our great people.

I'll hope to see you this Christmas vacation.

Love,

Older people writing to younger ones frequently feel the same gap as younger people do in writing to them. This is particularly true for nephews and nieces the writer doesn't know too well. If you're going to write such a letter, keep these suggestions in mind: Be good-humored; don't lecture; talk about things or people or events that will interest the reader.

Here's a short example of an uncle's letter to a niece he rarely sees:

Dear Amy:

Congratulations on your new job. Your father told me about how happy you were, and, of course, we're quite happy for you.

I ran into your friend Jim Bledsoe last week. He had lost about 40 pounds and was very proud of himself. He asked about you, and I thought he was a little in awe of your going off to the big city by yourself.

Your Dad mentioned that you're working with handicapped youngsters there. Did you know that the high school here has just begun a new program to bring handicapped students into the regular classrooms instead of segregating them in special classes? Apparently, everyone's benefiting: the handicapped kids are learning faster and the regular kids are learning to accept the handicapped kids as friends. I'm sending along a story about it I clipped from the paper.

I'd be interested in hearing about your reactions to the city, and about your apartment. Write me when you have some time.

Love,

ANNUAL LETTERS TO FAMILY AND FRIENDS

Do you envy the industry of those people who around each New Year send long, newsy, mimeographed letters about their family's activities? Do you wish you could pull yourself together to do the same thing? Here are some suggestions that can make it easier.

After you jot down all the items you think are important, and you find there's only enough to fill two or three paragraphs, stop. Then have a family meeting and ask the other members what they think should go into the letter. You'll usually find that everyone has different ideas about the year's outstanding events, and you should wind up with enough material for at least a couple of pages.

Don't censor yourself too severely. Let your letter contain news about the hard times as well as the good. You're trying to draw a reasonably realistic word-picture of the highlights of your year, not a fantasy about an ideal family that doesn't exist. Try to strike a balance: include some of the bitter along with the sweet. (It will make the recipients feel better to know that you have problems that match their own.)

If you still have trouble organizing a letter, here is a list of questions, the answers to which should provide you with more than enough material. If you ask each member of your family to answer these questions, you'll have enough to fill a book:

1. What are the two or three best things that happened to you this year?
2. What are the two or three worst things that happened to you?
3. What one or two places did you go to this year that stand out in your mind?
4. Did anything good or bad happen to the house you live in?
5. Did you make any major changes in the house?
6. Did your automobile involve you in any unusual expenses or adventures?
7. Did anything especially good or bad happen in connection with your job or your school work?
8. Did you have any illnesses worth mentioning?
9. Did you win any awards, honors, raises, prizes?
10. Did you make any major purchases, and if so, what effect have they had on your life?
11. Were there any important changes in your life this year?
12. Did you make anything that has given you or others pleasure?
13. Did you take up any new hobbies or pastimes? Did anything worth mentioning happen in connection with any hobbies you'd already been practicing?

Obviously, there's no end to the kinds of information you might put into a year-end letter, but this list should start you off well.

Organizing the Newsy Letter

There are several good ways to organize the information for an annual news letter. One is chronologically. The letter might begin like this:

Dear Friends:

It's been a terrific 12 months since we last wrote you. So much has happened that the only sensible way to tell you about it is to begin at the beginning. So, here we go.

January: All five of us picked ourselves up and went off to the Laurentians . . . .

The rest of this letter would have a month-by-month rundown of the family's activities. If you think this kind of outline is too detailed, organize by seasons instead, starting with the previous winter, then running on into spring, summer, and fall.

Another way of organizing your letter is to devote a paragraph to each person. For example:

Greetings, once again, from Billie, age 2; Martha, 7; John, 9; Shirley, 15; and Millie and Bert, the wonderful parents who shall be ageless.

We have triumphed once again over the forces of confusion and chaos, and will now bring you up to date on how we did it. Starting with the youngest.

Billie had a very close call this summer when a stray dog on the beach snapped at her and cut her just below the eye. The doctors said another quarter of an inch and we would have had very serious trouble. Fortunately, that quarter of an inch made all the difference—and she's now completely healed. Needless to say, we're keeping a sharp eye out for stray dogs these days.

Martha is our budding television performer. This fall she was chosen as one of five students to represent the youngest generation on a local television program

. . . You get the idea: each paragraph tells about one or two important events that happened to each family member during the year.

A third way to organize your letter is according to the activities in which the family is most interested. For example: places you've visited, childrens' school activities, job-related events.

Happy New Year from Joe and Mary Anderson, and Biff and Alice and Heinie the Cat.

Something new this year: We've met so many good friends we want to keep in touch with that we're undertaking this Annual Report to our Shareholders—that is, all of you with whom we share such a warm friendship.

The past year has been terrific/awful/dizzying/marvelous/wretched/delightful/great/unbelievable. Pick any of these—or all of them—and you'll be right. Here's why.

We went on several trips this year—once in the spring to visit Joe's mother in Boise. That was terrific because although she's now 83, she's as spry as a 20-year-old, and just as sassy.

In the summer we visited Yellowstone, where Alice, now 12, bumped into her current beau, whose family also happened to be there at the same time. We don't know how much she saw of Yellowstone, but she said it was the best trip she'd ever taken.

Joe's work and mine have both changed in some interesting ways. The firm he was working for folded in February—not to anyone's great surprise. For a couple of months, we were on beans more often than we liked, but in the spring, Joe landed a fine new job with a firm that's growing like crazy, and the prospects look wonderful.

I (Mary) finished my paraprofessional training as a teacher's aide, and have started working two hours a day at the elementary school across the street from us. I'm extremely happy to be back in circulation, and am thinking now of going back to school for a teaching certificate.

And now, for a few words about the children.

The rest of the letter will describe the children's activities and any other activities the writer feels are important.

A Personal Note

When you send the same letter to several people, add a personal touch to show that you're thinking of each recipient as an individual. Here are some of the kinds of things you might say:

How are all the children? Please write soon.

We miss you all and hope to see you before long.

When are you going to visit us? We're waiting impatiently.

5. Letters of Congratulation

In a good letter of congratulation:

1. Be reasonably short—unless you feel you really have a lot to say. (The point is, you're under no obligation to run on at great length.)
2. Mention the reason for the letter.
3. Be sincere.
4. Above all, show your good feeling for the recipient.

CONGRATULATIONS ON THE BIRTH OF A CHILD

Note how this brief letter fulfills the four points listed above:

> Dear Edie and Nat:
> Your mother has just told me the wonderful news about the birth of your twins.
> I guess the Good Lord felt there couldn't be too much of a good thing.
> I'm so happy for you both, and I wish you all the joy you both deserve.
>
> Love,

Here's an idea for a congratulatory letter on the birth of a child that the parents are guaranteed to save for many years—address the letter to the newborn infant:

> Dear Kid:
> I understand you've just arrived and that your parents haven't even picked out a name for you yet. Well, don't worry about that: you've chosen a couple of top-notch parents, and I think you'll find that they'll provide you with just about everything you need to lead a happy and healthy life (including a name all your own).
> Sorry I can't be with you to watch you grow up, but I've no doubt that you're going to become a wonderful person, just like all those others in your family.
> I'm sending along a small present which I hope you'll enjoy.
> And until I do see you, I want you to grow fast, be kind, and have a wonderful life.
>
> Fondly,

ENGAGEMENT CONGRATULATIONS

This congratulation also contains an invitation:

> Dear Sally:
> Congratulations on your engagement!

I'm looking forward to meeting your fiancé: if you selected him, I know he must be a grand person.

Can you and Jim come to visit us on Sunday afternoon, May 4th, around 3:00? We're having old Mrs. Barstow over at that time, and I know she'd love to see you, too. I hope you can say yes.

Cordially,

If you know both of the parties to the engagement, say something nice about each of them.

Dear Mildred:

Just read about your engagement. What fine news!

Carl is one of the most decent men I've ever known, and I believe you'll be extremely happy together.

I send my warmest congratulations.

CONGRATULATIONS TO A STUDENT

A youngster who's won a scholarship or a prize deserves appreciation. And since youngsters are concerned with their futures, they always like it when someone assures them that great days are ahead.

Scholastic Achievement

Dear Gwen:

We just read about your winning the Westinghouse Science prize, and were thoroughly delighted.

We've always known you to be an exceptional person; it's nice to see that the rest of the world is realizing it, too.

This is just the beginning of a long and fruitful career; I know you'll be both successful and happy in the years to come.

Athletic Achievement

Winners of athletic contests deserve a congratulatory message that they can add to their souvenirs.

Dear Bill:

Becoming State Tennis Champion at the age of 16 is pretty impressive. I'm very happy for you.

I know you've worked very hard, and that you often had to overcome some discouraging obstacles.

That you did it so well shows that you're a true champion. I'm sure that championship quality will help you all through your life.

Older Person's Graduation

Many older people are returning to school for advanced degrees or for special training. A letter to someone who's completed such a program might praise the person's character.

Dear Helen:

Some people are extraordinary. You're one of them; not only because you earned your degree in such a short time, but because you made up your mind to do it in the first place.

I think of how many people I know who simply let time pass them by; then I think of how you've taken time in your hands and made it work for you. And I realize once again how unusual you are.

You know that I wish you happiness and good fortune in the years to come. You surely deserve it.

BIRTHDAY CONGRATULATIONS

For Youngsters

Most people send birthday cards for greetings. If you want to be special, send a letter. You might make up an original greeting like this one:

Dear Billie:

T is for the terrific ballplayer you are.
W is for the wonderful jokes you tell—sometimes.
E is for everything you mean to your parents.
L is for the looney things you did last summer.
V is for the very idea of your almost being a teenager—who would have thought it!
E is for each day of your life: I hope they'll all be filled with delight. Happy birthday.

A more traditional birthday letter to a youngster might be a combination of newsletter and birthday greetings:

Dear Wendy:

Happy birthday! We wish we could deliver our greetings personally. But we send you our love directly from our hearts.

Since we saw you last summer, we've had a major change in our family. Sally has come home to live with us, having finished college in August. When I told her I was writing to you, she said, "Oh, send her my love. I do want to see her; she's one of the nicest kids I know."

Everyone in this house agrees with her. We hope to see you next summer. Until then, we send you our love and birthday greetings.

For Older People

A birthday greeting for an older person should be especially happy, simply because older people usually view their birthdays with some sadness at the passing of time.

Dear Bill:

There's a television commercial that says, "You're not getting older, you're getting better."

I suppose that, as with most commercials, there's a little bit of truth and a lot of salesmanship in it. But you're certainly getting better as you get older—as someone who's known you for a long, long time, I can be an objective observer on that point.

And since you were so good to start with, you're now getting to the point of being nearly perfect.

It's good to have a friend like that. Happy birthday, this year, and next, and the year after.

Or you might want to take a let's-face-facts approach:

> Dear Miriam:
>
> Aren't birthdays awful! They seem to say, "Another year has passed, and what have you done with yourself?"
>
> I have a better idea. Let's use birthdays to celebrate all the good things that are going to happen to us next year. So, instead of celebrating last year, on our birthdays we will be saying, "Whoopee! Here comes another year. What a bunch of good stuff's coming up."
>
> Let me begin the celebration by sending you one of the nicest things I have: my affection for you. Happy birthday, Miriam, and lots more to come.

CONGRATULATIONS ON A NEW JOB

When a friend gets a new job or a promotion, a friendly letter is a delight to receive.

> Dear Harriet:
>
> How lucky the Abex Corporation is to have got you! Do they know you're the most talented marketing specialist in the field? I suppose they must: everyone else does.
>
> I know you're going to make a tremendous impact on the firm. Good luck and happy times.

Sometimes you may want to send congratulations in order to pave the way for a future meeting. This is a combination social-business situation, which the following letter covers:

> Dear Mr. Harrison:
>
> I have a feeling that a lot of things are going to change for the better now that you're in charge of Monad Co.'s engineering.
>
> I'm not sure who's to be congratulated more: you for taking on your new job at Monad, or Monad for getting you.
>
> I know that you're interested in new ideas, and I have a number of thoughts I'd like to tell you about that you might find useful. I'll call you in a few days to see if we can set up a date.
>
> In the meantime, let me offer you my warmest wishes on your new position.

CONGRATULATIONS ON A PROMOTION

Letters congratulating someone on a promotion are similar to new job congratulations: in both cases, the person is taking on new responsibilities and facing new challenges. Essentially, the congratulatory letter expresses confidence that the person deserves the job and can handle the problems.

> Dear Tom:
>
> New York is finally getting a real sales manager. Congratulations on your new promotion.
>
> After so many years of training for the job in every part of the country, your marketing know-how has put you head and shoulders above everyone else in the company, and probably everyone else in the industry.
>
> The company will benefit from the enthusiasm and intelligence you've always shown, and I imagine that before long you'll be moving the whole firm into the number-one position.
>
> Go to it, and accept my best wishes.

CONGRATULATIONS TO AN ELECTION WINNER

If you believe in the candidate who's just won election to public office, let him or her know it. Voter support can do wonders to keep winners on their toes.

Dear Mayor Jordan:

Congratulations on your victory. As a voter who believes that you'll bring youth and integrity to the office, I want you to know that you'll have my full and vocal support.

The city needs your intelligence. I hope you'll pay special attention to the needs of the business community and the aged. You'll be hearing from me periodically; for now, I'll wish you the best of luck, and remind you that the hopes of thousands of people are riding with you.

DIVORCE

Perhaps congratulations is not precisely the right word to use when writing to someone who's just been divorced. After all, virtually every divorce involves a measure of sadness, because it represents a disappointed hope. On the other hand, divorce *has* become widespread. How can you best comment on it in a letter? Suggestion: Tact is called for, especially if you're not sure whether the recipient is happy or miserable. *Don't* say anything about the marriage, and *do* be kind. Ask yourself: what would be a nice thing to say or do for the recipient.

Dear Mary:

I've just heard about your divorce. I imagine that it will be a while before life gets back into regular and normal channels.

In the meantime, if there's any way I can help, you know you can call on me. We've been friends too long for you to stand on formality.

Let me make one specific suggestion. There's a new play opening in our town in about three weeks. It's supposed to be the funniest show in years. I'm going to get a ticket for myself, and I'd love to have company. Will you come with me? I'll wait until I hear from you before I go to the box office.

Cordially,

6. Acknowledging Congratulations

WHEN YOU'RE WRITING a letter acknowledging congratulations somebody's sent you, you should observe virtually the same principles that apply in writing a congratulatory letter: (1) be reasonably short; (2) mention specifically why you're writing; (3) be sincere; (4) show your good feeling for the recipient.

ACKNOWLEDGING BIRTH CONGRATULATIONS

The following letter may be longer than is absolutely necessary, but a new grandmother deserves a little extra.

Dear Mom:
    Thank you, so much, for your letter—and for the gift.
    The baby is thriving, and when she's not sleeping, she seems to be laughing.
    Now I understand what you meant when you used to say, "You can't understand how a parent feels until you're a parent."
    Marilyn and Tommy returned from the hospital three days ago, and now we're getting used to the round-the-clock routine of Tommy-tending. It's exhausting—but what a joy!
    We're planning on coming for a visit once things have settled down. You're going to be very proud of your newest grandchild. And your newest grandchild is going to be very proud of his grandma.
    Until then, we all send our love.

ACKNOWLEDGING WEDDING CONGRATULATIONS

When acknowledging wedding congratulations to a relative or friend who's known you a long time, it's nice to show that you remember past kindnesses.

Dear Uncle Bart,
    Your letter meant a great deal to me. Now that I'm starting on a new phase of my life, it's a comfort to recall the people who taught me about kindness and the importance of being a good friend.
    I'm sure that that knowledge is going to help me for the rest of my life.
    So, once again, thank you. And we'll hope to see you soon.

ACKNOWLEDGING WEDDING AND ENGAGEMENT GIFTS

A letter acknowledging a wedding or engagement gift can be brief, but should express sincere appreciation. It's polite to name the specific gift; otherwise, the acknowledgment is apt to sound a bit like a form letter:

Dear Jane:

Thank you, so much, for the lovely silver pitcher.

We have already used it several times. It dresses up our at-home dinners and makes us feel as if we're a very elegant couple indeed.

ACKNOWLEDGING A GRADUATION CONGRATULATION

The acknowledgment of a congratulatory letter from a friend can be short, as the one that follows shows. Or, you can lengthen it to give more news. The writing after the dotted line is an example of the kind of information that can be added once the basic acknowledgment is finished.

Dear Richard,

Your letter made me feel very lucky that I know someone like you.

It's true I'm pleased that I've finally managed to get the diploma, but the friendship we've had means more than any degree ever can. I want you to know that.

. . . . . .

I plan on leaving for New York next week to start job hunting. I'm going to be staying with Bill Crater, who tells me that he has an extra bed I'm welcome to.

If nothing turns up within a month, I'll be coming home for the holidays, and I'll hope to see you then.

Thanks again for your letter.

ACKNOWLEDGING CONGRATULATIONS FOR A NEW JOB OR PROMOTION

When people congratulate you on obtaining a new job or a promotion, let them know that you enjoy the work you're now doing. It helps them to feel good to know that you're feeling good.

Dear Mr. Masterson:

Thank you for your very kind letter.

The new job is challenging and exciting, and I think it will give me the chance to try some new ideas.

When you're in town, please call me. I'd like very much to have lunch or dinner with you.

Sincerely,

ACKNOWLEDGING CONGRATULATIONS ON AN ANNIVERSARY

As a general rule, in acknowledging any congratulatory letter, it's considerate to let the other person know that you value his friendship; after all, that's why he wrote you in the first place.

Dear Helen and Ben:

How nice it was to hear from you!

Our twenty-fifth anniversary came and went so quickly: it seems we barely had time to blink an eye and a quarter of a century had passed.

All things considered, neither Sam nor I can think of a better way we might have spent our lives. Especially when it's meant having friends such as you.

Thank you again for your letter. We hope to see you before too long.

7. Condolence and Sympathy Letters

CONDOLENCE LETTERS ARE usually very difficult to write. You want to express your sincere sympathy, but it's hard to put your sentiments into words that sound natural. The following suggestions may be helpful when you sit down to send someone a condolence letter.

1. *Before you write anything, think for a couple of minutes about the most important thing you want to say in the letter, and then about the next most important thing.*

For example, the most important thing you want to say might be that you send your sympathy. The second most important thing might be that you hope everyone feels better soon.

Or, the most important thing might be that you're sorry you're so late in sending the letter; and the second most important thing that you're glad the worst is over.

2. *Jot down these two important ideas.*

For example, using our first example, you might write down:

Send sympathy.
Hope you all feel better soon.

Using the second example, you might write:

Sorry I'm late.
Glad worst is over.

3. *Next, turn each of these notes into a full sentence, as though you were writing the letter.*

Example using the first pair of thoughts:

Dear Myra:
   I'm very sorry about your father's death.
   I hope the family will all feel better before too long.

Example using the second pair of thoughts:

Dear Byron:
   I apologize for writing you so late.
   I know Mary had a long and difficult illness, and I'm glad that the bad parts are over for all of you.

4. *Now put the letter away for at least a couple of hours.* When you come back to it, ask yourself, does it say what I want to say? If it does, send it. If it doesn't, you're now in a good position to add or delete ideas, or change the ones you've written.

This procedure won't make it a snap to write a condolence letter, but it will help you to organize your thoughts.

If you still have trouble, the following model letters may help you.

CONDOLENCES

On the Death of an Older Parent

If you can do it, it helps to say something nice about the deceased, however brief.

> Dear Jerry:
> I was sorry to hear about your mother's passing.
> Although I had met her only once, I recall her as an intelligent and lovely human being.
> I send you my warm sympathy.
>
> Sincerely,

On the Death of a Spouse

This is a letter that might be sent to a wife by co-workers of the deceased. With minor changes, it can also be a letter sent by only one person on his or her own behalf.

> Dear Veronica:
> Your husband's death is a sad event for all of us who knew him.
> We all held him in great respect and affection, and we shall miss him.
> All of us at his office send you our condolences; if any of us can be of any assistance, please call on us.
>
> Sincerely,

On the Death of a Child

The structure of this letter is useful for most condolence letters. First, it expresses sorrow; second, it says something about the deceased; third, it offers condolences.

> Dear Barbara and Peter:
> We were so very sorry to hear about Peter Jr.'s passing.
> We shall always think of him as we knew him: a delightful, intelligent person who made us feel young and good whenever we talked with him.
> He was a rare person, and we are very grateful that we had the luck to know him. We will always think of him as a living spirit of goodness and kindness.
> We send you our condolences.
>
> Sincerely,

SYMPATHY FOR AN ILLNESS

When someone you know has suffered a severely crippling illness, perhaps the most welcome letter you can send to the person responsible for the patient is an offer of sympathy backed up with an offer of help. The following letter offers general help; but if you can offer specific help, such as transportation or baby-sitting time, mention it.

> Dear Mrs. Moore:
> The news of John's severe illness saddened all of us.
> If we can help in any way, please call or write us and we'll do everything we can.

We know this must be a difficult time for you, and we want to assure you of our sympathy and our sincere hope that you will feel free to call on us.

Sincerely,

LETTERS TO SICK PEOPLE

The first—and about the only—rule for letters to sick people is: Be cheerful. Remember, when you're ill, you're worried about recovery and/or you're bored. Under those circumstances, happy letters are the only ones you want to receive.

Another point: Make the letter as long as you want. Sick people have little else to do, usually, than wait for recovery. The longer your letter, the longer they can be distracted from whatever's ailing them.

A Sick Child

Children love riddles, puzzles, jokes, and games. This is a good example of a letter that provides them. Also notice that at the end it suggests topics for the child to write a letter about. Children often have difficulty in thinking of what to write; and this letter solves the problem.

Dear Marlene:

I was very sorry to hear that you're sick. The only thing I can think of that is worse than being sick is having a test in school for which you haven't prepared.

Here's a riddle: What has 18 legs and catches flies? Give up? Here's the answer, in secret code: maet llabesab a.

To figure out the code, read the answer backwards.

Now, I'll give you something else to keep you out of trouble. Here's a sentence with blank spaces in it. Fill in the first blank with any word in column 1. Fill in the second blank with any word in column 2. And fill in the third blank with any word in column 3.

Once upon a time there was a _____ who was very bad. So all the _____ shouted at it and punched it until it got better. Now, it is always very _____

Column 1	Column 2	Column 3
child	people	happy
monster	monsters	sad
monkey	bushes	nervous
rich man	chickens	tall
poor man	apricots	sick
banana	telephones	wobbly

Everyone in our family is rooting for you to get better quickly. So please do.

And if you feel like writing to us, we'd love to hear from you. Here are some questions we'd like you to answer:

1. What does your doctor look like?
2. Do you like her?
3. What's your favorite joke or riddle?
4. What's your favorite dessert?

Write us soon.

Love,

Victim of a Serious Accident

When writing to someone who's had an accident, be sympathetic and cheerful. Sending along a funny or an interesting newspaper item is an easy way to make the patient feel better. In this letter, the material between the dotted lines is an example of the kind of family news that a sympathy letter might also include, if it seems appropriate. Naturally, news of any other kind that will interest the patient could just as well go in here.

Dear Chuck:

The news of your accident came as a terrific shock.

I haven't yet learned the details, but I wanted to let you know right away that I hope you recover quickly.

The world needs you too much for you to stay in bed one minute longer than you have to.

I'm enclosing a newspaper story that will give you a chuckle.

. . . .

The family has been doing some interesting things lately. My sister, Martha, just got a job with the city school system helping children with severe hearing problems; it's something she loves doing and that she's very good at, so naturally she's very happy about it.

My father went through a tight period a month ago: he was laid off at his shop because his company went into bankruptcy. But fortunately he landed a new job within a couple of weeks, and it looks as if he's going to be doing pretty much the same kind of work for the same kind of money.

. . . .

When you're able to drop me a line, please do. Until then, I hope you get better and better every day in every way.

Sincerely,

An Invalid

Here's an example of a cheerful letter to an invalid. Its only purpose is to amuse the recipient, and it makes no pretense of seriousness. You probably won't send this letter to someone who's suffering from a grievous illness, but rather to someone who simply has to be confined for a convalescence.

Dear Anne:

Now that you're confined to bed for a while, here are some suggestions for passing the time:

1. Think about all the aggravation you're missing at your job. Add it all up and put it away in your treasure chest: when have you ever been so lucky?
2. Make a list of all the terrible parties you've been to in your lifetime. Think of how happy you are they're behind you now, instead of ahead of you. Give yourself a pat on the back for remarkable achievement in terrible-party survival tactics.
3. Spend half an hour reminiscing about all the men you barely escaped getting serious with.

By the time you're finished, you ought to be sufficiently happy to jump out of bed in half the time you expected.

Do get well quickly.

Love,

8. Acknowledging Condolences, Death and Funeral Notices

CONDOLENCE ACKNOWLEDGMENTS ARE generally of two types: formal and informal. The formal ones are usually printed and folded so that the sender can add a personal note on the undersheet.

A standard printed or engraved card looks like this:

Mr. William Smith
wishes gratefully to acknowledge
your kind expression of sympathy.

The card may have a black border if you wish, or it may be plain. Naturally, the person or persons doing the acknowledging may be listed individually or collectively. So, instead of "Mr. William Smith wishes gratefully to acknowledge your kind expression of sympathy," it might be appropriate to say:

Mr. and Mrs. William Smith
wish gratefully to acknowledge, etc.

If children are acknowledging the death of their only surviving parent, the card might read:

The children of
Mr. William Smith
wish gratefully to acknowledge, etc.

Informal acknowledgments may vary in length from one to several sentences. Here are some typical examples that might be sent to someone who has offered condolences:

Thank you for your kind letter. I am [or: The family is] very grateful for your thoughtfulness and sympathy.

That letter will be suitable to send to almost everyone who offers condolences. You may, however, want to personalize some of the letters a little more. A short note is all that's necessary.

Dear Mr. Waters:
    The family appreciated your very kind letter. Dad always spoke highly of you. Your letter makes us feel proud that he had such a fine friend.

What kind of stationery should you use for these acknowledgments? Any standard stationery is suitable. Plain white or subdued gray is a satisfactory color.

DEATH AND FUNERAL NOTICES

When preparing a classified ad for insertion in a newspaper, provide the paper with the following information:

1. Last name of deceased
2. Given name of deceased (also maiden name, if a woman)
3. Address of deceased
4. Date of death
5. Age of deceased at time of death
6. Names and relationships of survivors
7. Time and place of interment
8. Whether services are private or open to friends and relatives
9. If flowers are not wanted, add: "Please omit flowers." Or insert a sentence such as: "Memorial contributions to [name of organization] preferred."

The complete notice can read as follows:

Anderson, May (née Bullums), of 37 A Street, Newark, suddenly on June 12th, in her 45th year, beloved wife of Harry Anderson and mother of Mary, John, and Howard. Funeral services at Community Church, 39 Franklin Street, Tuesday, June 15th, at 3 P.M. , followed by interment at Central Cemetery at 4 P.M.. Relatives and friends invited. Please send memorial contributions to the American Cancer Society.

9. Thank-you Letters

A PLEASANT LETTER of thanks for a favor—or any other nice thing someone's done for you—is a superb way to show friendship. As with all personal letters, the key to a good thank-you letter is to make it honest. It needn't be long or flowery.

FOR A WEEKEND

When thanking people for a weekend, mention some specific feature that will please your hosts: their children, their pets, their cooking, for example.

> Dear Jim and Marge:
> It was a wonderful weekend. Seeing you all again was pure pleasure.
> Joe and I both feel that your Joey and Jill are about the best-mannered and best-natured youngsters we've ever seen—I suppose they must have learned from their parents.
> We'll hope to see you again before long.
> > Love,

FOR AN INTRODUCTION

When you thank people for arranging an introduction, consider whether they'd like to know what's resulted from it. This letter deals with that kind of situation.

> Dear Helen:
> It was very kind of you to arrange my introduction to Dr. Ebbingkraft.
> I met him last week, and he said that he thinks he'll be able to give me a number of useful suggestions.
> I do appreciate your help, and I'll keep you informed if anything interesting develops from it.

FOR AN INTERVIEW

After a job interview, a brief letter of thanks may help strengthen a favorable impression. Notice that this letter not only thanks the interviewer, but also suggests that the writer would *want* to work hard if awarded the job. It's a subtle point that can help make the interviewer more favorably disposed to the letter writer.

> Dear Mr. Ruthven:
> Thank you for the time you spent with me yesterday.
> Your description of the career opportunities at General Amalgamated made it sound like a place where employees *want* to contribute their best; I found that very appealing.
> I look forward to hearing from you.

FOR ASSISTANCE

When someone spends time guiding you around town, or around any place, for that matter, a short letter of acknowledgment can help create a warm glow. If you mention something your guide was especially attentive about or proud of, it will give your letter extra warmth. This letter, for example, does it with the sentence "The bits of history . . . ."

Dear Joel:

You are a terrific guide.

By the time I got ready to leave, I felt I knew the campus forwards and backwards. The bits of history you mentioned really made the place come alive for me.

I appreciate the time you spent with me, and the friendship you showed; it went far beyond anything I had expected.

If there's any way I can help you, please tell me.

In the meantime, until we get together, I send you my warmest regards.

FOR SERVICES RENDERED

Sometimes you may want to send a letter to a stranger who's helped you in a difficult situation: perhaps someone who assisted you when you had a flat tire, or who came to your aid during a health emergency. The letter of acknowledgment that follows is suitable for these circumstances. Note two points: It expresses a personal emotion of gratitude, and it tastefully mentions a small present that the sender is giving. If no present is being sent, that paragraph can be omitted.

Dear Mr. Bindler:

I want to thank you once again for helping me last Sunday.

Your kindness to a stranger in distress was simply wonderful.

It made me feel—as I have rarely felt before—that what is most important in life is helping other people. I guess that's what being human means.

I'm sending a small gift as a token of my appreciation, and I hope you'll accept it in the spirit of friendship with which it's offered.

Again, thank you.

Sincerely,

FOR A PARTY

Thank-you notes for parties are a pleasantly civilized gesture that makes the party giver feel it really was worthwhile.

Dear Jocylin:

What a fine party you throw!

Everything was grand: the food, the drinks, the atmosphere, and especially the pooplo.

I had a lovely time. Thanks so much for inviting me.

As ever,

10. Requesting Information and Offering Opinions

IN THIS CHAPTER, we'll deal with the situations you face when you have to cope with a large, impersonal institution, such as a government agency or a company. Further on, we'll give some model letters, but to begin with, here are some basic principles to help guide your letter writing.

1. *State the reason you're writing in the very first sentence of your letter.* The people who will read your letter are probably overworked and underpaid, and they don't have the patience to read through a long letter. So always state the reason right at the beginning.

Here are a couple of suitable typical first sentences:

Dear Sir:
   Can you send me your catalog?

Dear Sir:
   Please send me a copy of my birth certificate.

After that first sentence, you may want to explain yourself further; but hit them with your main punch right at the beginning.

2. *Include all relevant reference numbers and dates.* If there is any likelihood that the information you want is filed under a certain number or date, include it in your letter.

For example, if you're writing to a company about a bill, an invoice, or a missing shipment, include such things as the number on the invoice, the date you bought the item, and the address of the store where you purchased it.

Today, most business and government operations are run by numbers. If you give them the numbers they need, they will be able to help you much faster.

3. *Confine your letter to discussing one point only.* For example, you may want to offer a newspaper editor your opinion about a public issue. If you want the letter to get serious attention, stick to that one issue. When recipients read a letter that deals with two, three, or more subjects, they get confused because they don't know where to focus their attention.

If you have a number of things to write about, write a separate letter for each.

4. *If you want the recipient to take some action, say so, very clearly and specifically.* The last paragraph of a letter is often a good place to do this.

Here are some typical examples:

Please send me a copy of the material I've requested.
Please send me a refund and a personal apology.
Please send me a corrected copy of this record.

It's vitally important to spell out exactly what action you want the recipient to take; if you fail to make that clear, the recipient may play it safe by doing nothing.

5. *Make your letter as short as possible.* Include nothing that isn't absolutely necessary. The reason: The more unnecessary information you put in, the more likely the recipient will get bored and fail to take you seriously.

Except in the most extreme necessity, never let the letter run more than a page. And after you write the first draft, put it aside for a few hours, then pick it up and see if you can cut out a paragraph or even a line. Every extra word is litter that hurts your letter.

6. *If possible, write to an individual.* If you don't know whom to write to, you may be able to find out with a telephone call. If you're still not sure of whom to write to, send your letter to the top person in the organization. That person may not read it, but it will be sent to the correct person with a memo to take care of it. And when the right person sees a memo from the boss, he's more likely to give your letter prompt attention.

7. *Make sure your letter is legible.* This point, which should be obvious, apparently is not, since one of the commonest reasons why institutions answer letters improperly, or fail to answer at all, is that they can't read the handwriting. If you can, typewrite. If you can't, use your best handwriting, and if your best handwriting is as bad as mine, print.

If you follow these principles, there's a good chance you will get the right people to pay attention to you and answer your questions or carry out your requests. Now, here are some model letters which you will find helpful in putting together your own letter.

OFFERING AN OPINION

When you want to offer your opinion to a government or private organization, your letter should make three points: (1) your opinion; (2) the reasons behind your opinion; (3) what action you think the recipient should take.

Here's a model letter with brackets and blanks, followed by an example of the same letter with the blanks filled in.

Dear Mr.
   I think the Department is [doing right or wrong] in [following a specific course of action].
   The [course of action] will [help or harm] people like me who are [explain your interest in the subject].
   My reasons for believing the Department is [acting well or badly] are:
First,
Second,
Third,
   For these reasons, I believe you should [explain the action you want taken].

A letter based on the above model might read as follows:

Dear Mr. Johnson:

I think the State Department is acting unwisely in urging that all students undergo a week of cultural orientation before visiting overseas countries.

As a student, I think the policy would be quite harmful to me, and would actually hurt our national interest. Let me explain a few of the most important reasons why I feel this way.

First, if I plan to visit several countries, I'd have to get oriented to all of them, and I simply don't have the time.

Second, when I go abroad, I'm never sure of where I'm going until I get there.

Third, the program would be very expensive to run, and I think there are more important things that taxpayers' money can be spent on.

I urge you to forget about this program, because it is unworkable, unnecessary, and costly.

Sincerely,

REQUESTS FOR INFORMATION

Requests for information should be short and specific. Include information that you think will help the recipient give you exactly what you want.

Gentlemen:

Please send me a list of government publications on running a small business.

I am planning to open a haberdashery in my town, and will appreciate any information dealing specifically with that subject.

Dear Sir:

Can you give me an explanation of Line 24 of Commerce Department Form 238AA: Equal Opportunity Employment Calculation?

Specifically, does Line 24 refer to all employees or only to those in the office?

Please send me your explanation as soon as possible.

Sometimes you will want information that the recipient may not want to give you. For example: A public official or a company may be doing something that affects your neighborhood adversely, and you may be gathering information that will enable you to stop it.

Your letter should be firm and polite. Do *not* get involved in an indignant, angry exchange because the likelihood is that indignation won't get you anywhere. Indignation can be useful at the right time, but not when you're trying to gain information. To illustrate the point, here are two letters about the same matter:

Letter One

Dear Sir:

I am outraged that your company is planning on putting up one of its restaurants in our neighborhood. We're a residential area and we don't need any fast-food concessions ruining the place.

What's your authority for thinking you can come in here and just build in any district at all whenever you like? And what kind of building license are you operating under?

Letter Two

Dear Mr. Johnson:

As a resident of the South Side, where your company is about to erect a new restaurant, I would appreciate it if you would provide me with this information:

1. The number of the city construction permit under which you are operating.
2. The names of any other agencies or individuals from whom you have received written permission to proceed with construction.

Thank you for your cooperation.

LETTERS TO THE GOVERNMENT

Asking a Favor

While government bureaucracies tend to be impersonal and often downright inhuman, they are staffed by human beings as well as by computers. When asking a favor, be specific about what you're requesting, and give clear reasons why you think your request should be granted. Here's an example of a letter that might have been sent to the Justice Department:

Dear Mr. Levi:

If you could grant my husband, William Bender, a release from the Albany Federal Prison a month earlier than he is eligible, I would be very appreciative.

I make this request because both his mother and his father are now in the hospital, and are suffering from terminal cancer.

The doctors say that neither of them is likely to survive another two months. But my husband is not eligible for release for another month and a half.

To prevent him from seeing them before they die seems to me to be needlessly cruel.

My husband has been a model prisoner, and the parole board has recommended that he be released on January 1.

I am requesting that he be freed immediately, about a month earlier than that.

Will you please give permission for his release, and let me know how soon we may expect him home?

Again, I shall be most grateful for your help.

Sincerely,

Mrs. William Bender

P.S. My husband's serial number in Albany is 023−45−172

Health and Drug Inquiries

Letters to government agencies relating to health and drug matters should be as specific as possible. If you're asking about a chemical or drug compound, include any of the following information that is relevant:

1. The kind of product
2. Brand name
3. Name and address of manufacturer, packer, or distributor (these appear on the label)
4. Code marks or symbols (may be embossed on ends of cans or on labels)
5. Name and address of the store where you bought the article
6. Approximate date of purchase

Here's a letter that incorporates all of these items:

> Dear Sir:
>   I am writing to ask whether it is safe to use the circulatory drug Isomerl.
>   The drug is made by L. R. Sifon Co., Albemarle, Texas. The code number on the label is S-45671.
>   I bought the bottle about a year ago from my local druggist, P. S. Richardson, of Main Street, Marlboro, Massachusetts.
>   Since then, I have been told that the drug has been condemned.
>   Please let me know if the government has made any statement about the possible danger of this product.
>   Sincerely,

If you're writing a similar letter to the company that made the product, the only change needed would be to eliminate the sentence, "The drug is made by the L. R. Sifon Co., Albemarle, Texas."

Here's another letter of inquiry. Note that the major question appears in the first sentence.

> Gentlemen:
>   Are vitamins sold by discount mail-order companies safe?
>   Further, is the labeling reliable?
>   I have a catalog that offers such vitamins, and the prices are quite attractive. The catalog is issued by W. M. Meredith Co., Orange, Kentucky.
>   Please let me know if I may safely buy the vitamins in this catalog.

Educational Benefits

We repeat the rule we've given time and time again in this section: When corresponding about any personal matter that may involve numbers, give all the numbers you can think of.

> Dear Sir:
>   Do you offer educational benefits to the children of veterans who died in the line of duty?
>   My husband, Paul Ankers, Serial No. 476—231, died on active duty in Vietnam in 1970.
>   Our two children, Paul Jr. and Mary Ann, will soon be going to college. Naturally, we are interested in obtaining any benefits for which they are eligible.
>   Please send me any information about the eligibility of children of veterans.

PENSIONS, COMPENSATION, INSURANCE

Pension, compensation, and insurance letters should always carry relevant serial numbers, claim numbers, policy numbers, and any other numbers you can find that might be helpful.

It's a good idea to place them at the top of the letter, on the right side, like this:

> Serial No. 123456789
> Case No. 98765432
> Claim No. 12/34/90

Premiums

Gentlemen:
Please tell me when my next premium is due.
My policy number is C—222.

Pensions

Give all the information the recipient might need in order to give you an enlightening answer.

Dear Sir:
Can you tell me if I'm eligible for a veteran's pension?
I served in the U.S. Navy from January 15, 1944, to March 23, 1946.
My serial number was B 34—87—2929.
I am now sixty-two years old and in poor health.
Please let me know about my eligibility.

ARRANGING AN INTERVIEW

When you want to set up an appointment with a business executive or a government official, be brief and to the point. You can probably do it in four sentences, as in this letter, which (1) requests the appointment; (2) explains the reason for the request; (3) shows how to fulfill the request; and (4) ends politely.

Dear Mr. Anderson:
Would it be possible to have a brief meeting with you at your office in the near future?
I'm Safety Chairman of the 12th Street Association, and I should like to discuss some new ideas for reducing the hazards posed by some of your trucks in our neighborhood.
If it is possible to arrange such a meeting, would you be kind enough to let me know when it would be convenient?
I know your company's reputation for good citizenship is well earned, and I'm looking forward to meeting with you.

Sincerely,

CHANGES OF ADDRESS

When notifying a company or government agency of a change of address, include your old address as well as your new one, and, of course, any relevant serial or policy numbers.

Dear Sir:
Please send all future compensation checks to my new address:
Wehey Road
Maspeth, Va.
My former address was:
23 Ardrey Street
Foxboro, Wash.

Sincerely,

11. Answering Those Inquiries

WHEN A COMPANY, a government organization, or any other institution sends you a letter that you plan to respond to, observe the following suggestions:

1. Your first paragraph should mention the letter to you, giving the date and the general subject matter.
2. Your second paragraph should answer the letter as briefly as possible.
3. In additional paragraphs, try to give all the information requested, but don't give any more than is asked for.

LETTER TO AN INSURANCE COMPANY

If the information requested is too long to fit neatly in the letter, enclose a list.

Dear Mr. Geresy:
    Your letter of January 15th asks me to itemize the goods that were damaged in the fire that destroyed our summer home.
    I'm attaching the list to this letter, giving the approximate price of each item.

        Sincerely,

LETTER TO A COMPANY

If you're including a few brief facts in your letter, list each one in a separate paragraph and put a number in front of each. This makes the letter easier to understand.

Dear Mrs. Margitay:
    In your letter of March 17, you ask for details of my idea for an improved clothespin.
    There are three elements to my idea which make it an improvement over conventional clothespins:

1. It can be manufactured for about half the price of clothespins now on the market.
2. It has a new clip that holds clothes more firmly than any existing clothespin.
3. It is made out of a material that will withstand extreme temperature changes.

    If the idea interests you, I'll be happy to bring you my drawings.

LETTER TO A GOVERNMENT AGENCY

When the government asks you anything about your financial affairs, keep these things in mind: first, before answering, get the opinion of your lawyer or accountant—if you have one—on how you should answer; second, if you have neither, give absolutely no more information than is requested. What they don't know can't hurt you.

Gentlemen:

This is a response to your letter of September 3, in which you ask for an explanation of my income.

All my income is salary, as reported on my Federal Income Tax returns.

Sincerely,

LETTER TO A SCHOOL

If the letter you're answering lists several questions, answer them in the order in which they were asked.

Dear Dr. Abbington:

Thank you for your letter of May 15th. I would, indeed, be interested in teaching at Londonderry during the summer.

Here are my answers to your questions:

1. I will be available to teach on Wednesdays, Thursdays, or Fridays, in the mornings or the afternoons. If it's a matter of indifference to you, I would prefer the afternoons.
2. I would be able to provide the class with all the raw materials needed, at a cost of about $25 per student.
3. The fee you suggest sounds a bit low to me, but we can discuss it when we meet, and I'm sure we'll come to a satisfactory arrangement.

I look forward to meeting you when you're in the city next month. Why don't you plan on visiting my studio for tea at about 4:00 any weekday?

Let me know what day will be convenient.

Sincerely,

FRANK LETTERS

Sometimes a request calls for a frank answer. Remember, you can be frank without becoming angry or emotional. For example, if a store's prices have been consistently high and it asks for your business, you might answer with a letter like this.

Gentlemen:

You recently sent me a letter asking why I had failed to place my customary order with you for Christmas fruit packages.

The answer is that your prices are out of line with your competition.

Admittedly, the quality of your products and the reliability of your service are both first rate. But so are those of your competitors.

Therefore, I have chosen to do business with them this year.

If you can bring your prices more in line with other companies selling similar items, I'll be glad to consider buying from you again next year.

Sincerely,

SENDING DOCUMENTS

Never let an original document out of your hands if you may need it later. Send a photocopy. And check the photocopy before you send it to make certain that the important information is legible. Here's a letter that deals with that problem:

Dear Mr. Frober:

Thank you for your letter of March 12.

You ask whether I have a receipt for the damaged pen which I sent to you.

I am enclosing a photocopy of the postal receipt.

The serial number is not clear on the copy. It is: 345–678.

Sincerely,

12. Complaint Letters That Get Action

WRITING A GOOD complaint letter is often difficult because people tend to let their emotions get in the way of what they want to accomplish. Frequently they're angry, and they let that anger control the letter. This is always a mistake: uncontrolled anger usually diminishes the force of a letter.

If you really feel you have to write an unbridled letter of complaint, by all means write it and get it off your chest. Then put the letter away.

Now, write the letter you're going to send. Here are some points to keep in mind before setting pen to paper.

Think carefully about the best person to write to. For example, if you've had a credit problem with a department store, don't write to the credit department—write to the president of the company. (See Chapter 1 for a discussion of this point.) In general, when writing to any institution, address your letter to the boss.

Keep copies of all your correspondence. This is especially important when you're writing complaint letters because in later correspondence, you may need to remember exactly what you said—and when.

Make up your mind not to be sarcastic or insulting. Sarcasm and insults may satisfy your rage, but they often act as an obstacle to achieving your goal. Put yourself in the other person's place. If you got a letter that called you an incompetent or worse, your reaction would be: "The heck I am!"—or worse. Such a letter would probably make you uncooperative.

So, keep your complaint letter factual, and if you want to express outrage or anger, try to direct it at the situation you're in, rather than at the person you're writing to. That way, you stand a chance of enlisting the recipient's interest in your terrible plight.

ORGANIZING A LETTER OF COMPLAINT

Now, let's organize the letter by organizing your ideas.

1. Write down what you want the recipient to do for you; that is, the action the person should take in order to remedy the complaint.

2. Write down why you think it's important to have your complaint remedied.

3. Write down any information the person needs in order to take the action you want taken.

4. Write down anything you believe you can do to encourage the recipient to take that action—this includes any kind of pressure or threats you believe will be effective.

You now have the basis for your letter of complaint. Let's see how you might develop such a letter for a typical complaint.

Suppose you live in an apartment and the intercom between your house and the front door doesn't work. You want to write a complaint letter to the landlord demanding that it be fixed.

Following our suggestions, you'll first write down what you want the landlord to do for you:

I want him to repair my bell *now.*

Second, write down why it's important:

It's been inconvenient; it's been out of order three weeks.

Next, write down any information the landlord needs in order to remedy the complaint. Some of the things he might need to know are:

I'm home every morning, so his people can come in.
The last time it was repaired, it broke down after a week—maybe there's something wrong with his workmen.

Fourth, write down anything you can think of to encourage the landlord to fix the bell:

I'll report the matter to the rent control commission if it's not fixed.
I'll refuse to pay any more rent until it's fixed.
It's unsafe living in an apartment without an intercom.

Now, you're ready to write a first draft of your letter. Put each of those points in a separate paragraph. It will look like this:

Dear Mr. Fasiello:
Please have my bell repaired immediately.
It has been out of order for the past three weeks, and I have been seriously inconvenienced.
Your people can come in any morning of the week to do the necessary work in my apartment. Incidentally, the bell broke down within a week after it was repaired the last time: perhaps you should check the quality of their work more closely.
If the bell isn't fixed within the next week, I'll have to report the matter to the city rent control commission.
Please send someone to fix the bell at once.

Sincerely,

A couple of points should be mentioned.

First, notice that the letter ends pretty much the way it began: with a request to get the bell fixed at once. This intentional repetition helps to emphasize what you want done. It may not always be possible, but generally, you'll find it a good practice to end your letter with the same request with which you began it.

Second, notice that the letter used only one of the points we had listed under the fourth section—ideas to encourage the landlord to fix the bell. When you write your letter, you'll find that you want to subtract ideas—or add them—as you go from basic outline to first draft.

Remember, as we said in the first chapter of this book, have plenty of scratch paper so that you can freely try out different ideas and words and discard the ones you don't like.

Now, let's look at some models of typical complaint letters. When you have to write one of your own, examine these first; you may be able to find paragraphs from different models that will help you in putting yours together.

COMPLAINT ABOUT FRAUD

If you feel someone has victimized you and you want to complain to an authority, here's a model letter you can follow. It might serve as a letter to a company president if you are complaining about a salesman; or to a government agency, such as the Federal Trade Commission, if you feel a company has been fraudulent in dealing with you.

The organization of the following letter differs slightly from the organization suggested at the beginning of this chapter for other kinds of complaints. For this letter, here are the steps to follow:

1. *Describe the problem.* If you bought something that was misrepresented, include copies of the advertising or labeling. If someone told you a lie, summarize what was said.

2. *Identify the name and address of the person or the organization you're complaining about.*

3. *Explain why you think the practice is misleading or unfair.*

4. *If you're complaining to a federal government agency, explain why you think the merchandise or the practice you're complaining about involves interstate activities*—since the federal government can usually interfere only in interstate cases.

Dear Sir:

I should like to register a complaint about a fraudulent pricing.

On November 9th, I went to buy a Little Dandee Electric Knife Sharpener at your store at 14th and Main streets.

The salesman on duty claimed that the Dandee was being sold at a specially reduced price of $10, which was 50 percent lower than the normal retail price. I bought the sharpener. I am enclosing a copy of my receipt.

A few days later, I found the same machine being sold in another neighborhood for $7. The storekeeper there told me this was the standard price for the Little Dandee.

I think that your salesman deliberately misrepresented the price on this merchandise to me.

I plan to send a copy of this letter to the Attorney General's office, and another copy to the Federal Trade Commission, with the request that they follow the matter up.

However, if you will send me a refund of $3—equal to the amount I was overcharged—I shall consider the matter closed and will take no further action.

Sincerely,

COMPLAINTS ABOUT CREDIT AND CHARGE ACCOUNT ERRORS

When you get involved in a problem about a charge account or credit card, it's often because of an error generated by the company's computer equipment. A clerk may have entered the wrong number into the computer, and the computer simply did as it was told—and you wound up with an overcharge or some other sort of error.

The best way to cope with these problems is:

1. *Always write immediately to the president of the company.* This increases the chances that your letter will receive careful attention.

2. *Avoid emotionalism.* It will obscure the purpose of your letter.

3. *Give all the relevant facts needed to clear up your problem.*

4. *Send along photocopies of any documents you think may be helpful in proving your point.* Never send originals.

Here's a model letter:

Account 045–32–189

Dear Sir:

I recently received a statement from your company for $250. The amount is not correct.

As you will see from the enclosed photocopy of the receipt, the item I bought was $150.

Please send me a correct invoice.

Sincerely,

COMPLAINTS TO INSURANCE COMPANIES

Many problems with insurance companies stem from computer errors. In trying to get them corrected, you have to give all the facts. The following letter gives the facts and describes in detail precisely what the writer wants the company to do:

Identification No. 307–41–41
Case No. 45–897–23
Patient: Mary Carthus
Date of Service 3/13/74 to 4/3/74

Dear Mr. Raggi:

Your letter of July 19 denies benefits because you say our child, Mary, "is not a student and is over 19 years of age."

Your records are in error.

Mary is ten years old. She was born June 24, 1964, as a review of your records will certainly show.

Please, therefore, do the following things:

1. *Acknowledge receipt of this letter* by a personal acknowledgment, not a computer-written letter or card.
2. Acknowledge that you are correcting your records to show Mary's correct birthdate.
3. Acknowledge that a check for the benefits due will be forthcoming.

Several months have passed since this claim was entered. Your company's delays and errors are outrageous. If the matter is not settled within the next 30 days, I shall complain to the Better Business Bureau, the Attorney General, and the State Commissioner of Insurance.

Sincerely,

A couple of additional points are worth noting about this letter. The writer saved the anger for the final paragraph, after carefully presenting all the facts. This helped to concentrate the force of the anger.

Second, asking for a handwritten acknowledgment is a good idea because it increases the chances that the problem will be handled by a human being, not by a machine.

COMPLAINTS ABOUT A DEFECTIVE PRODUCT

When writing to a company about a defective product, keep the letter short and to the point. And as we've said repeatedly, don't bluster: it only arouses resentment.

Your letter should include the following information:

1. Model number.
2. If you don't have the model number, a detailed description of the product.
3. Name and address of the store where you bought it.
4. Date of purchase.
5. It may also be useful to include a copy of the bill of sale and copies of paid invoices for any service that's been rendered on the product.
6. A short description of the problem.
7. If you've written before about the problem, give the date of the most recent letter you've had from the company and the name of the person who signed it, so that it can be easily found in the company's files.
8. Companies often put a file number on their correspondence. Usually it's at the top or bottom of the first page and it may carry a notice such as: "When corresponding about this matter, please refer to File No. So-and-so." When you write to the company, put: "Your File No. So-and-so" at the top of your letter.

Your File No. 123 – A

Gentlemen:

I believe you have made an error in your letter of January 15th.

You say that the warranty on my electric can opener expired last year.

If you will reexamine the date, I believe you will find that the warranty still has two years to run: The opener was purchased in 1976, and the warranty will expire in 1981.

Please make the necessary repairs, and return the machine postage-paid, as your warranty says.

Sincerely,

It may be useful to put your complaint in positive terms—to tell the company that you expect it to live up to its usual high standards.

Dear Sir:

I know that your company has a reputation for quality products and fairness toward its customers. Therefore, I'm writing to ask for a replacement for a defective lawn mower.

I purchased the machine about a year ago at the Watchung Discount Center, Watchung, Nebraska. I'm enclosing a photocopy of a canceled check used to pay for the machine.

It is a 1.5-horsepower Cuts-Ezee, Model 2356.

A month after I bought the machine, the engine failed, and I had it repaired under the warranty.

Since then, I have had the engine repaired three more times—twice under warranty, and once after the warranty had expired.

Now the engine has broken down again.

I have already spent more than $30 in repairs, and I am beginning to seriously question the quality of your mowers.

I am requesting a replacement of this machine with a new one.

I hope that you will live up to the standards for fair dealing on which you have built your success.

Sincerely,

COMPLAINT ABOUT OVERCHARGE

When you send a letter complaining about being overcharged, cover the following points:

1. Review the problem briefly.
2. Request a specific action, that is, a refund or a credit.
3. Provide any helpful documents.

Dear Mr. Smith:

I trust you will be able to correct an overcharge.

On November 13th, I bought a sofa and two chairs at your store.

Your salesman told me shipping charges would be $17.00. I paid him for the chairs and the shipping.

When the driver delivered the chairs, he told me there was a $15 additional charge.

I paid that, too, although I did tell him that I was sure there was an error.

I am enclosing a photocopy of the receipts for the furniture and the shipping, and for the extra $15.

I feel that the extra $15 charge is most unfair, if not downright dishonest. I'm sure you'll agree that a refund is due me.

Will you please send me a check for the $15.

Sincerely,

COMPLAINT ABOUT INCORRECT BILLING

When you're billed incorrectly for any product or service, your letter of complaint should state all the relevant facts. If it will be helpful, include additional facts that will clear up any confusion.

Gentlemen:

Your statement of February 12 is incorrect. It lists a charge of $12 for bed-sheets.

Although I ordered the bedsheets, I have not received them. Therefore, I am sending you a check for $15.75—the amount of the statement minus the $12 charge.

Please correct your records.

Sincerely,

COMPLAINT ABOUT AN UNPLEASANT INCIDENT

From time to time, you may want to write a complaint about an unpleasant incident you've been involved in. It might be a run-in with a clerk in a store or an employee of a company or an agent of some sort. The following letter will serve as a model.

Note that the first sentence states the reason for the letter. A list of the important facts immediately follows: This is a good way to state the facts quickly and clearly. Next, there is a brief description of the event. And finally, there is a paragraph on the action the writer wants taken.

Taxi Commission
87 Beaver Street
New York, N.Y. 10005
Attention: Investigations Dept.

Gentlemen:
 I wish to register a complaint about a cab driver. Here are the essential facts.

 Date of the incident: Wednesday, February 25
 Time: About 5:45 P.M.
 Place: Southeast corner, 15th St. and Second Ave.
 Cab License No.: 6404 TA
 Driver's Last Name: Crissman; First name: Unknown.
 Description: White male, about 25. Reddish-blond beard.

 Description of the event
 There were four passengers: myself, my wife, my daughter, and my mother-in-law. When we reached our destination at 15th St. and Second Ave., the cab stopped.
 I got out, as did my mother-in-law and daughter. Then, while my wife was half out of the cab, it started and knocked her to the street. She cried out and the cab stopped. I helped her up.
 I told the driver I wanted his number. He refused to give it to me and started the cab. I had my hands on the cab, and running alongside, urged him to stop. He accelerated and I was knocked to the street. He continued driving off.
 I sustained bruises when I fell. My wife was also bruised.

 Action I would like taken
 I think the driver should have to undergo further training in driver technique. His starting the cab while the rear door was open indicates that he doesn't know his job, and that he needs to be taught those basics if he's going to continue as a cab driver.
 Sincerely,

COMPLAINT TO GOVERNMENT REPRESENTATIVES

Keep your letters to your congressman, senator, or any other government official as short as possible. When you have something to complain about, state the nature of the complaint in your first sentence; give any necessary further information in your second paragraph; and in the third paragraph, say what action you want taken.

Above all, restrict your letter to one issue: If you write about a string of unrelated grievances, your letter won't get the serious attention it deserves.

Dear Senator Mason:
 I strongly oppose your position on gun licensing.
 I think there are three overwhelming reasons why we need a strong gun-licensing law:
 First, right now, anyone can buy a gun and kill with it.
 Second, the number of gun-caused deaths in this city has risen by ten percent a year for the last five years.
 Third, every major law enforcement official in the state has come out in favor of strict control.
 I urge you to vote in favor of the new gun control legislation. If you fail to do so, I shall definitely vote for your opponent in the next election.
 Sincerely,

13. Responding to Complaints

You MAY FIND it necessary to answer a complaint by mail. Perhaps a neighbor has complained about your child or your dog, a company about nonpayment, or a landlord about the noise from your apartment. The question is: How can you deal with these complaints intelligently and effectively?

Every situation is different, of course. But here are some suggestions that may prove helpful.

1. *Before you write anything, think.* Decide what the real nature of the complaint is. If someone has sent you a letter of complaint, read it carefully so that you're sure you understand precisely what he thinks is wrong.

The reason for this caution is so you will avoid getting upset about something that the complainer hasn't actually said. Therefore, when you answer, you'll be discussing the real issues.

2. *Think about what you want your letter to accomplish.* Do you want to tell the other person to jump in a lake? Do you want to offer a full apology? Or, do you want to strike a note that's somewhere between the two? Once you've decided on that, you're well on the way to framing your letter.

3. *If the person who wrote you the letter is a member of a large company, or anyone who may not know exactly what you're replying to, summarize his or her letter at the beginning of yours.*

> Dear Mr. Johnson:
>
> In your letter of January 17th, you say that I am $35 in arrears on my payments.

If the letter has a file or serial number on it, write that in at the top of your letter, as described on page 45 of this book. This will insure that the person you're writing to is able to figure out quickly what you're referring to.

4. *Even if you are sure the recipient will know immediately what you're writing about, it may be a good idea to summarize the issue in your first paragraph.* This will help the other person to understand how you see the issues—always useful when two people are discussing a difference between them.

> Dear Mr. Anderson:
>
> You believe that we have built our garage on your property.

This kind of opening is not always appropriate, but often it's a good, easy, clear way to begin.

5. *Make your major position clear in your next paragraph.* Are you going to apologize? Are you going to argue? Are you going to ask for more facts? Are you going to

take some action as a result of the complaint? Express your position here. Here are a couple of examples, building on the two samples we've already started:

> Dear Mr. Johnson:
> In your letter of January 17th, you say that I am $35 in arrears on my payments.
> I am very sorry that this has happened and I plan to start paying again, immediately.

In this case, the most important things the writer wants to express are an apology and a promise to begin payments. The letter might have gone differently:

> Dear Mr. Johnson:
> In your letter of January 17th, you say that I am $35 in arrears on my payments.
> I think you'll find that your records are incorrect. My last payment was made to you just two weeks ago.

In this case, the writer felt that the most important thing was to set the record straight. Now, let's look at the other letter we've started.

> Dear Mr. Anderson:
> You believe that we have built our garage on your property.
> We believe you are mistaken. Our deed shows that the garage is clearly within our property lines.

In the above letter, the writer sets down the most important fact as he sees it: the writer of the complaint letter is apparently mistaken. Under other circumstances, the second paragraph might read:

> Dear Mr. Anderson:
> You believe that we have built our garage on your property.
> We are having our lawyers check the deed, since it was our understanding that we were building entirely within our own property.

In this version of the letter, the writer is answering the complaint with a soft reply and a description of the action being taken to deal with the complaint.

All of these examples follow the same basic structure: they immediately tell the reader the most important piece of information that the writer wants to get across.

6. *Write down additional information that you believe will justify your position or explain your attitude more fully.* Keep it as short as you can reasonably make it; eliminate irrelevant details, old grudges, etc. Your letter will be stronger if you stick to the main issues.

Let's see how our apologetic late-payer might continue:

> . . . I am very sorry that this has happened, and I plan to start paying again, immediately.
> Illness in the family caused us to fall behind, but we are making a special effort to catch up, and we shall be fully up-to-date within another couple of weeks.

The alternative version of the letter might go this way:

> . . . I think you'll find that your records are incorrect. My last payment was made to you just two weeks ago.
> If you will check your files again, you will probably find a record of payment.

In the case of the property dispute, the letter might continue:

> . . . Our deed shows that the garage is clearly within our property line.
> It may be helpful to you to know that our records on this property go back some 200 years, so we are reasonably certain that we are correct.

In this case, the writer used historical documentation to bolster his argument. The alternative version would use a different approach:

> . . . We are having our lawyers check the deed, since it was our understanding that we were building entirely within our own property.
> Of course, we realize that some of these old boundary markers are unclear, and before we come to any conclusion, we'd like to do a little more research.

Here, it's a soft answer that should gain time until more facts can be determined.

7. *Write down what action you plan to take, or what action you want the recipient to take.* This will usually be the last paragraph of your letter.

For example, in the late-payment apology, the final paragraph might go like this:

> . . . We will certainly try to keep up-to-date on all our payments from now on.

The alternative version might go this way:

> . . . If your files show that you have not yet received my payment, please let me know, and I'll take steps to get a new check sent to you.

The property letter might conclude this way:

> . . . We'll be happy to show you our records, and to compare them with yours. If you'll call us, we'll be glad to set up a time to get together.

And the alternative version could have an ending that shows the writer is a friendly, cooperative person:

> . . . We know that you're quite concerned about this, and so are we. We should hear from our attorney shortly, and we'll be in touch with you then.

Now, let's look at some responses to other kinds of complaint letters.

APOLOGIZING AFTER A COMPLAINT ABOUT A CHILD

A neighbor complained about the misbehavior of a child. The parent wrote this letter of apology. Note that it follows the basic outline suggested above: a summary of the complaint; an expression of the writer's attitude; a brief further commentary on that attitude; and a concluding paragraph about future action.

> Dear Mr. Christopher:
> I agree with you that Billy's behavior last weekend was unacceptable.
> I want personally to apologize to you in this letter. On our next trip to the country, Billy will come personally to apologize.
> We have talked with him at some length about what he did, and why it was wrong. He understands now, and I believe that he will never do it again.

I appreciate your speaking to me directly about this matter, as I think it will help us to prevent future episodes.

Sincerely,

TURNING ASIDE A COMPLAINT ABOUT A CHILD

Here's the same situation as in the previous letter, but a different answer. In the following letter, the writer expresses sympathy for the complainer's situation, but stops far short of an apology. At the same time, the letter is not cold or insulting.

Dear Mr. Christopher:

I'm very sorry that Billy's behavior last weekend upset you.

We have discussed the situation with him and have told him of your feelings. Billy, too, regrets that you were upset.

As he explained it, the boys have been using the field for several years, and none of them knew that you objected.

Billy has promised that he will not play in the field again.

Sincerely,

ANSWERING A COMPLAINT FROM A TENANT

In this letter, the landlord apologizes and suggests a course of action that may create better relations in the future. But apologies are not the only possible course of action, as the sample letter after this one shows.

Dear Mr. Trotta:

Last week you told my agent, Mr. Tobin, that you were going to withhold your rent because you were not getting adequate heat in your apartment.

I'm very sorry that you were inconvenienced.

We have been having a lot of trouble with the boiler. We recently managed to replace some important parts, and we think it will work satisfactorily now.

If you feel that the heat is insufficient, will you please call me and let me know, so that I can take steps to remedy the situation?

Sincerely,

NONAPOLOGETIC ANSWER TO A TENANT COMPLAINT

Dear Mr. Trotta:

Last week you told my agent, Mr. Tobin, that you were going to withhold rent because you were not getting adequate heat in your apartment.

Naturally, I'm sorry that you feel that way.

We do try to keep the apartments at a minimum temperature of 68°, and we apparently have been quite successful, since we've received no comments like yours from other tenants.

As you know, we have checked the heating pipes in your building and they are working efficiently.

Therefore, I suggest that you do the following things:

When you feel cold, make sure that your windows are all shut.

Check your thermometer when you think the apartment is too cool. If you do keep a record, perhaps we can track down the problem, if one does indeed exist.

In the meantime, I want to encourage you to not to withhold your rent, since it would simply involve us both in legal problems we don't want.

Sincerely,

In this letter, there's no apology; there is, rather, an implied threat of legal action, but it is softened by the attempt to be helpful.

ANSWERING A COMPLAINT ABOUT NOISE

People do have parties, and sometimes they do get boisterous, and if you want to maintain good relations with complaining neighbors, one way is to apologize graciously—and soon.

Dear Mr. Bellamy:
We're very sorry that our party last Saturday night disturbed you.
We had not expected that it would get quite so loud—and I'm afraid that we didn't pay too much attention to the volume, since we were spending most of the evening running around as host and hostess.
Naturally, we're especially regretful that we kept Mrs. Bellamy awake; we have always had a very high regard for her, and would want to do nothing that would harm us in her estimation.
We certainly will be more sensitive to your feelings in the future, and we do hope you'll forgive us this breach of good neighborliness.
Sincerely,

ANSWERING A COMPLAINT ABOUT PETS

Accidents will happen that are beyond our control. If you take full responsibility for them, it can help ease the way over a difficult period while relations are reestablished.

Dear Ms. Johnson:
When we learned that Jenny had dug up your garden, of course we were dreadfully upset.
We know how much it means to you, and how much work you put into it. That we were indirectly responsible for so much damage is very distressing.
As you know, we have always made it a practice to keep Jenny on a leash. We can only guess that she escaped because the person taking care of her wasn't familiar with her tricks.
We do want to make amends when we return in three weeks. In the meantime, once again, let us assure you that we're deeply concerned, and that we will do everything in our power to see that it doesn't happen again.

ANSWERING A PUBLIC COMPLAINT

People engage in a number of outdoor activities that others object to: motorboating, hunting, and skimobiling are accused of being noisy, dangerous, and harmful to the environment. When people write letters to the newspapers complaining about these activities, here's an example of a civilized response that can be offered:

To the Editor:
In your March 12th issue, Mrs. Berman C. Coolidge wrote a letter complaining about "barbarian motorboaters" on Lake Muskeag.
As one of the barbarians, and as the owner of a 15-foot outboard, I'd like to comment.
Lake Muskeag is a recreation center for all the people. There are strictly enforced laws governing where the boats may go—and not go. They may not go

near the swimming areas that Mrs. Coolidge enjoys. So she is safe from us.

But we, apparently, are not safe from her. I am sorry that she wants to do away with all motorboating on Muskeag; we motorboaters do not want to do away with swimmers like Mrs. Coolidge.

We are all living in this world together, and there is room for all of us—if we show tolerance.

Mrs. Coolidge, I extend the hand of tolerance to you; will you do it to us?

Sincerely,

ANSWERING A COMPLAINT ABOUT PERFORMANCE

When someone for whom you've completed a job complains that it's unsatisfactory, there are several courses open to you, and the following letters suggest some of the alternatives. First, if you're willing to redo the job, say so, willingly and cheerfully. To do it grudgingly can only increase the other person's irritation. To do it graciously can ease matters considerably.

Dear Mrs. Molloy:

I am very sorry that you are not happy with the work that I did on your home.

Naturally, I want you to be completely satisfied, and I will do whatever is necessary to make you completely satisfied.

I expect to be free in another two weeks, and at that time I'll call you and we can arrange to complete the work to your full satisfaction.

Sincerely,

You may feel that you've done your job properly and that the other person is taking unfair advantage of you. Answer cheerfully, but protect yourself by suggesting that additional work will require additional money.

Dear Mrs. Molloy:

I'm very sorry that you're dissatisfied with the work I did on your house.

I'll be happy to make any changes you'd like.

There will, of course, be a charge for any additional time and materials that are required.

Under the terms of our agreement, your final payment constituted your agreement that the work was satisfactorily completed.

Please call me at any time to discuss the additional work you feel you'd like to have done.

14. Résumés and Job Application Letters

THINK OF A résumé as a sixty-second television commercial: that's probably all the time the reader is going to spend on it. If he or she is interested in what you've written, you may be able to sell yourself in a personal interview.

How, then, can you present yourself most effectively in a résumé whose main purpose is to persuade the prospective employer that you're the best possible person for the job? In this chapter, we'll offer many suggestions. Let's tie them to reality by discussing an actual résumé.

(1)
William C. Hartnett
414 West Mason Street
Missionary, N.Y. 12345

(914) 333–9999

(2)   Résumé of Working Experience

(3)   1975–Present   (4) Operations Supervisor
                       (5) Missionary Clothing Corp.
                       Missionary, N.Y.

                       (6) Supervise staff of three production people. Responsible for scheduling production and coordinating it with other departments. Also, handle some personnel problems and do employee motivation work.

                       (7) Have been in this position for two years, and have helped to increase productivity about 20% and decrease absenteeism about 15%.

       1973–1975   Operating Engineer
                       Pirks Corp.
                       Dartmouth, Mich.

                       Responsible for managing most of the manufacturing equipment in a plastics manufacturing factory. Work required regular maintenance of equipment and advising on repair and purchase. As a result, became knowledgeable in the buying of a wide variety of machines.

1971–1973	Parts Manager
	Kleban Manufacturing Co.
	Prisko, N.D.

    Maintained and distributed an inventory of about 8,000 parts for a large, diversified manufacturing operation. (8) Helped organize the inventory system so that it could grow easily and efficiently to three times its present size.

Education

(9) College:
    Breedon Community College
    Orangeville, Ala.
    B.A., 1969

Special:
    Myers Technical Institute
    Mason City, Mich.
    1973–1974
        Courses in production, machine maintenance, and computer technology

High School:
    Breedon High School
    Breedon, Ala.

Service Record

1968–1970
    U.S. Navy
    Enlisted as Apprentice Seaman,
    Honorable Discharge as Machinist's Mate,
      2nd Class

Personal

(10) Marital Status: Married
Health: Excellent
Height: 5'10"
Weight: 170

Honors and Affiliations

(11) 1973:   Gold medal winner, AAU Wrestling Olympics
1972:   Silver medal winner, Michigan Wrestling Assn.
Member: Dartmouth Little League, Dartmouth Presbyterian Church

References

(12)   Available on request

ANALYSIS OF THIS RÉSUMÉ

1. *The person's name, address, and telephone number are at the top of the résumé where they can easily be seen.* They may be positioned in the middle, as here, or on the left or right side. The point is that this information should be immediately visible.

2. *The title, "Résumé of Working Experience," is only one possible title.* You might prefer "Résumé," "Experience," "Summary of Working History," or "Professional History." Some people prefer to use no title.

3. *Chronological organization of working experience:* The common way to organize a résumé is with your most recent job listed first, and your first job listed last. In

dating your first entry, it's better to use the word "Present" than an actual date because you may want to use the same résumé over a period of a couple of years.

4. *Job title:* List the job title first because, generally speaking, a prospective employer is more interested in you than in the company you worked for. Since you want to put your best foot forward, give yourself the best-sounding title you can think of that describes your job.

5. *Company name:* It's not necessary to put down the street address, but giving the city or town adds a realistic, factual tone.

6. *Describing your work is usually the hardest—and the most important—part of making up a résumé.* Here are a couple of suggestions:

If your company has a written job description of your work, you might use this as the basis for your résumé description—especially if you feel it will make your job look more important.

Think about the kind of person who's likely to make the decision on whether to hire you. What does he or she probably want in a new employee? Lots of experience? Enthusiasm? Imagination? Reliability? Whatever it is, that is the main thing to stress, not only in your description of your present job, but also in your descriptions of all your other jobs. In this résumé, for example, all the job descriptions are written so that they emphasize the applicant's management skills: they talk about scheduling, coordinating, handling personnel problems, purchasing, and organizing. You may not be able to make all of your jobs fit neatly into this pattern, but if you're aware of what you want to do, you'll be able to do it better.

Try to make your responsibilities on each job sound different. If you just repeat three times that you were a draftsman, the reader will feel your experience is limited. But if you list mechanical drafting on one job, engineering drafting on another, and marine drafting on a third, you'll seem much more experienced.

7. *Whenever you can, provide some information about your successes and achievements.* Ask yourself: What recognition have others given that my work is unusually good? If you can't think of anything, don't lie—but if you do probe your memory, you may be pleasantly surprised.

8. *Dress your work in golden colors.* Many relatively simple tasks can be made to seem more important. For example, consider the statement: "I helped organize the inventory system so that it could grow easily and efficiently to three times its present size." This could mean merely that he shifted boxes and bins around so that more boxes and bins could be piled on top of them.

The point is, don't lie in a résumé, but on the other hand, don't neglect to put yourself in the best possible light.

9. *List all educational degrees you've received.* If you haven't received any, you should still put down the name of any institutions you've attended, including dates of attendance.

10. *"Marital Status," "Health," "Height," and "Weight" are optional.* If for some reason you'd rather not mention them, it won't hurt you to leave them out.

11. *"Honors and Affiliations" is a catch-all heading under which you can list items not covered in the rest of the résumé.* The honors may be any awards you've earned that distinguish you from everyone else and show your superior qualities. Even if the

honors are unconnected with your work, put them in, because they show that you're a person of unusual abilities.

Your affiliations are often important, especially if they show that you're involved in your community. If your affiliations are with highly controversial or unpopular organizations, it is probably best not to mention them.

12. *If your references are famous, it may pay you to mention them.* Otherwise, there's no point in including them here: you can give them when you're called in for an interview.

OPTIONAL INFORMATION

Job Objective

Some people think it's a good idea to include at the top of the résumé, just below your name, the heading "Job Objective," with a short descriptive title, such as:

Job Objective		Job Objective
Shop Foreman	Or:	Field Salesman

The advantage of this is that it focuses the reader's attention on the specific job you're interested in. However, you may not know exactly what job you're interested in, or you may prefer to leave the matter less definite. If so, it's safer to omit the heading.

Salary Desired

Some people believe it's a good idea to put down the desired salary at the head of the résumé. It is probably a bad idea. If you desire a salary lower than they're prepared to offer, you're losing money. If you desire a salary higher than they're prepared to offer, you may lose a job that might soon pay the salary you want. It's generally a better idea to wait until you have an interview to discuss salary.

Style

The language in most résumés follows one of three styles:
It may be written in the first person:

I worked as a sales manager, in charge of a force of 12.

It may be written in the third person:

He worked as a sales manager, in charge of a force of 12.

Or it may omit the personal reference:

Worked as a sales manager, in charge of a force of 12.

If you use the first-person form, try to reduce the use of "I" to a minimum so that the résumé doesn't sound too egotistical.

The third person "he" strikes some readers as pretentious. On the other hand, it is a convenient way to avoid the tiresome repetition of "I."

Omitting the personal pronoun, as in the third example, is a good, safe style, although it may sometimes appear too abrupt.

Whichever style you finally choose, read the final wording aloud to yourself to see if it sounds natural and easy. If it sounds good to you, it will probably sound equally good to a prospective employer.

SKILLS RÉSUMÉ

While the chronological résumé is satisfactory for many people, you might consider another form, the skills résumé. This résumé emphasizes the different kinds of experience you've had, and eliminates any mention of when you had them.

This kind of organization is often useful for professionals who have had many jobs, and for people who've been in one job for a very long time and have handled a variety of assignments.

Here's a portion of a résumé used by the author of this book: Notice that it's written in the third person, to avoid the repetitive use of "I."

Representative Projects

Sales Meetings: For Eastman Kodak, Mr. Blumenthal wrote a one-hour mixed-media presentation which explained the new Pocket Instamatic camera to photofinishers. Delivered by top Kodak executives at an industry meeting in Chicago, the presentation helped the company write more than a million dollars in sales in the first 24 hours.

Training Programs: For Chase Manhattan Bank, Mr. Blumenthal wrote an audio-visual training program that is now being given to most clerical employees to upgrade the quality of their work. For the Commonwealth of Pennsylvania, he prepared a five-session presentation on boating safety now given to virtually all small-craft boat owners in the state.

Employee Programs: The American Express Credit Card Division was concerned about high employee turnover. Mr. Blumenthal was retained to analyze the problem and suggest solutions. Following his recommendations, the division instituted a multimedia orientation program for new employees. Mr. Blumenthal also helped design a special conference room to house the program.

Organize the Paragraphs for Your Audience

All of the paragraphs in the résumé above were organized to intrigue prospective clients. Here's a list of some of the principles involved:

1. *Name-dropping.* Seeing the names of large corporations comforts people. They feel that if you've worked well for large and successful organizations, you may do equally well for them.

2. *Results-oriented.* Where possible, assignments have been described in terms of their successful outcomes. Thus, in describing the Eastman Kodak assignment, the million dollars' worth of sales was mentioned.

3. *Breadth of experience.* Since the goal is to give a picture of wide experience, each item leads off with a different category of assignment; for example, sales meetings, training programs, employee programs. Without these headings, the presentation would have had much less impact. The headings provide specific points on which the reader can focus.

4. *Problem-solution format.* Sometimes it's possible to explain how you solved a client's problem. The résumé's example of American Express is a good case in point. When you tell the reader: "Here's a problem," his or her reaction is likely to be: "What's the answer?" In other words, the problem-solution format is a good way to keep the reader's interest.

If you're a young person with not too much working experience, you can still write a résumé that will make prospective employers think: "Wow! This kid looks great!"

RÉSUMÉ FOR YOUNG PEOPLE

Naturally, it will take some thought, and some careful organizing. Start out by drawing up a list of five kinds of experience.

1. *List all the jobs you've ever held—part-time, full-time, whatever.* Write down a brief description of what you did:

Life Guard: Jones Beach. Summer, 1974, 1975. Helped save three people.

2. *List the subjects you've majored or minored (if pertinent) in at school, that you think might help you in your work.*

3. *List scholastic and athletic honors, and other forms of recognition you've won, such as scholarships or grants.*

4. *List extracurricular activities and positions of prominence you've achieved in any groups you belong to:* Were you a captain, a treasurer, a vice president?

5. *List your college fraternity or sorority.*

Once these are listed, use them as the basis for your résumé. It might look something like this:

Résumé of
Wilma Martin
240 Minor Street
New York, N.Y. 10001
Telephone: (212) 999−9999

Objective
Market Research

Scholastic Record
1972−1976   Boston University
Boston, Mass.
Bachelor of Arts, 1976

Majored in Marketing
Scholastic Average: B plus

Minored in Music
Scholastic Average: A

Work Record
1972−1976   Various part-time sales and marketing jobs including: sales jobs in book stores, department stores, and door-to-door.

Market Research: Did survey research work both on and off campus for Doremus Research, Inc. Also handled tabulating and analysis of results of about two dozen surveys.

Extracurricular Activities
Boston University Band: 1972−1976
Manager, Boston University Chamber Ensemble, 1975−1976:
Booked dates and handled publicity for this group, which traveled to ten cities while I was managing it.
Sorority: Chi Phi Pi, Honors Society of Music Dept.

Honors and Recognitions
Academic scholarships, 1973, 1974

Marborough Prize, 1975: Awarded for outstanding essay dealing with contemporary political subject.

Americanism Award, 1972: Awarded by the Brookline (Mass.) American Legion.

Personal

Marital Status: Single

Health: Excellent

Height: 5'9"

Weight: 130

References

School, working, and personal references available.

COVERING LETTERS

The covering letter that you send along with your résumé can help you land the job you want. In this section, we'll describe two kinds of covering letters: general letters sent when you don't know the recipient, and letters sent to specific people.

In both cases, perhaps the most important thing to think about as you write your letter is: What is the recipient likely to want from an employee?

For example, if the recipient is hiring sales people, he or she might be most interested in a prospective employee's ability to meet the public, past record of achievement, or ability to open new accounts. If you believe you know which one of these features your prospective employer is most likely to be interested in, emphasize it in your letter. If you don't know, then build the letter around the significant quality or qualities you believe you possess.

Here's an example of a general letter that might be sent to a group of prospective employers:

Dear Sir:

During the past five years, I've been helping one of the city's major companies to clamp down on some of its most rapidly rising costs.

As the enclosed résumé explains, I've worked as bookkeeper on a wide variety of assignments.

While I can look forward to a secure career in my current job, I'm interested in more than security: I enjoy finding new problems to solve, and new challenges to overcome.

Having a deep respect for the profit system, I know that high productivity is one important key to profits. I can offer both high productivity and a careful attention to detail.

I plan on calling you next week for an interview to see whether you can use my skills as a bookkeeper.

Sincerely,

If you're a beginner in a field, and thus have no experience to speak of, emphasize your personal qualities:

Dear Sir:

The ability to learn quickly, the desire to do a first-rate job, and a willingness to put in as much time as is needed to see the job through are some of the qualities I can offer an employer.

I'm especially interested in factory operations, and I have a number of skills I think would be useful to your company.

I'll call you next week to arrange an interview to discuss job opportunities with your company.

Sincerely,

15. Effective Letters of Reference

SOMEONE HAS ASKED you to write a letter of reference. What do you say in the letter? What should you say if you think the person is wonderful? What should you say if you think the person is not so wonderful? And what should you say if you think the person is terrible?

Let's pose a different problem: Suppose you've asked someone to write a letter of reference for you and that person says he'll be glad to write whatever you want him to. What should you suggest he put into the letter?

Since the answers to all these questions rest on the same simple principles, we can discuss them together.

1. *The letter should answer the questions the reader is likely to ask.*

In some cases this is easy: The recipient may simply be interested in knowing about the competence or character of the person.

In other cases, however, the recipient may want a great deal of specific information. This is particularly true when the letter is being written to an institution of higher education or to a professional organization that may be interested in several different aspects of the person.

So, before you write the letter, check to see whether specific kinds of information are requested.

2. *Be complete, but be discreet.* This means be honest, but don't overpraise. Extravagant praise may make the reader wonder just how objective you're being.

3. *Be specific.* When you're commenting on someone's abilities, give specific examples of what you mean.

For instance, instead of saying: "John Smith works well with children," you might say: "John Smith has a great deal of patience with difficult children; they seem to sense his affection for them, and they return it."

4. *Don't say what you don't know.* If you're asked to write about certain aspects of the person's character or experience with which you're not familiar, it's usually better to come out and say so, with a phrase such as: "I have not had an opportunity to observe . . . ." Another alternative is simply to ignore aspects of the person's work you're not familiar with.

5. *Identify yourself.* Explain your relationship to the person for whom you're writing the letter.

6. *Make appearances count.* The more businesslike your letter looks, the more good it will do for the person you're writing about. A typed letter on letterhead stationery is probably best. If you write the letter, be sure that your handwriting is easy to read.

7. *Don't be afraid to say no.* When you're asked to write a letter of reference for someone you can't say anything good about, there are two options. You can say no, politely, offering whatever diplomatic or undiplomatic excuse you wish. Or you can write a letter that is honest, but sufficiently restrained so that you can live with your conscience. Further on, we'll provide an example of both kinds of letters.

ENTHUSIASTIC LETTER OF REFERENCE FOR A JOB

The following commendatory letter covers several points: it carries a warm personal endorsement; it describes how long the person has worked for you; it praises his abilities and his motivation; it is specific about his job skills; it mentions his ability to get along with a group; and it explains the reason for his leaving.

Dear Mr. Anderson:

I am happy to recommend Richard Jones to a prospective employer.

Richard has worked for our company for five years, and we have a high regard for his abilities and his motivation.

As a bookkeeper, he has always been careful, neat, and accurate.

His character and personality are commendable; he has always worked well with his colleagues and his superiors.

We were most unhappy that the elimination of his department made it necessary to release him. But we believe that his next employer will be acquiring an efficient, productive, and cooperative employee.

Sincerely,

ENTHUSIASTIC REFERENCE FOR A STUDENT

Letters of reference for students should emphasize the sterling qualities of character and personality that will make the admissions officers feel the student is going to be a credit to the school. Here are two examples. The first one is a general, all-purpose letter of recommendation.

To whom it may concern:

As a friend of her family, I have known Shelley Bergen for the past ten years.

She is a spirited, intelligent young woman, and I believe that any institution will benefit in many ways from her presence.

Among the personal traits she possesses, the following seem to me to be most prominent:

She is an independent thinker. She likes to consider all the facts of an issue and then make up her own mind.

She has a good understanding of people. She has always been able to make friends with people of any age and economic status; in short, she is open to the world.

She is a serious person. She is modest, but she believes that what she is doing is important and worth doing well.

She is a most unusual young woman, and I believe she will make a useful contribution to the college she attends.

Sincerely,

This next letter of reference for a student is more specific. If you can give similar examples of good behavior, it will help strengthen your letter.

To whom it may concern:

Richard Hobart is a young man whose unusual character will, I believe, make him an asset to any school he attends.

I have known Richard for about six years, and have found his character to be exemplary. It may be useful, however, to give an example of the kind of person he is.

Not long ago, some war orphans from a foreign country were placed in our community. Richard decided to help them. He spent about twelve hours a week with them, teaching them English, taking them on tours around our area, introducing them to his friends. He did this voluntarily, never asking for—or receiving—public recognition for his efforts.

While this is an outstanding example of his sense of social responsibility, it is not unique.

I know Richard will benefit from his college experience; I believe, equally, that the college he attends will benefit from his presence.

Sincerely,

A LESS ENTHUSIASTIC LETTER OF REFERENCE FOR A JOB

The following letter of reference is the kind you might write for an employee who has done an adequate job, but not much more than that.

Gentlemen:

Richard Jones has worked with us for five years.

He is a competent designer who understands the major principles of his work.

With proper supervision, we are confident that he will perform his work quickly and faithfully.

Sincerely,

REFUSAL TO GIVE A LETTER OF REFERENCE

Suppose someone writes to you and asks either for a letter of reference or for permission to use your name as a reference. And suppose you feel that you can't give the person a good reference. How should you respond? Here's one way:

Dear Mrs. Jacobsen:

I'm sorry that I cannot give you the reference you ask for. [Or: I'd prefer that you did not give my name as a reference.]

The problems that arose about your work here may have been peculiar to this company. Perhaps they will not occur in a new job.

You'd probably agree that you deserve a fresh start, unbiased by any carryover from us.

For that reason, I think it would be best if you did not use us as a reference.

Sincerely,

LETTER OF REFERENCE FOR A PUBLIC POSITION

You may want a friend or a colleague appointed to a position of honor or public importance, perhaps to a committee investigating certain public issues, or as the judge in a local contest or a member of the board of directors of a local museum. The letter you write in his or her support can emphasize one or both of the following: (1) the person's general ability and qualifications; (2) the person's interest in, and support of, the particular activity for which he or she is being recommended. The following letter gives both:

Dear Mayor Jansen:

In selecting a director for the city's Centennial Celebration, I recommend that you consider Ms. Angeline Mayakov, vice-president of the city Chamber of Commerce and owner of Angeline's Restaurant, 423 Baker Street.

Ms. Mayakov's qualifications for this position are outstanding. To cite just a few of them:

The Centennial Celebration will need a superb administrator, and Ms. Mayakov is exactly that. She started and created what is now one of the most successful restaurants in this city.

The Centennial Celebration will need to involve all city groups, and Ms. Mayakov probably knows more people and has been active in more groups than almost any other resident. She is a past president of the Chamber of Commerce, and has held office in at least a dozen other civic and business groups, including the Daughters of the American Revolution and the National Organization of Women. She is active in church affairs, and is popular among the youngsters because of her Little League sponsorship.

The Centennial Celebration should be directed by someone who loves the city. Ms. Mayakov has shown her love many times—most recently by her generous donation for trees on major business streets.

The Centennial Celebration will need someone with imagination to direct it. Ms. Mayakov has imagination: her initiation of ethnic street festivals during the summer months is only the most recent example.

For these reasons—and for many more—I urge you to consider Ms. Mayakov for this position. I know her only slightly, and have no personal stake in her appointment. But I believe that all of us will benefit if she is placed in charge of the celebration.

Sincerely,

LETTER OF REFERENCE FOR AN HONOR

Gentlemen:

This year, as you review possible recipients for the Man of the Year Award, I urge you to consider William Morris, of 123 Bayside Avenue.

Mr. Morris is not rich, famous, or powerful. But his achievements make him one of the outstanding citizens of the state.

Mr. Morris has devoted much of his adult life to helping comfort the aged and helplessly ill. He has done this selflessly and generously, at considerable personal expense, and virtually without publicity.

Mr. Morris is now 55 years old, and the father of a family of four.

For the past ten years, he has spent four evenings a week visiting the homebound people of his neighborhood—mainly those who have been neglected and forgotten by almost everyone else.

He has read to them, talked with them, brought them food and medicine. He has helped some of them regain health, and he has overseen the burial of others.

Mr. Morris works in the post office as a mail sorter, a position he has held for 15 years. But his real job is that of helping those who need help most.

We who sign this letter are his neighbors. We are not the only ones who urge that you choose him as Man of the Year. Attached is a list of the names, addresses, and telephone numbers of 50 people whom he has been helping over the past couple of years. They, too, urge you to consider him as this year's Man of the Year. We can think of no one who has ever deserved it more.

Sincerely,

LETTERS OF INTRODUCTION

A letter of introduction is like a handshake on paper. It's written to introduce one friend or business associate to another. Generally speaking, there are two kinds of letters of introduction: one that you write to your friend or associate introducing someone who'll be coming to visit; and another that you give to your visiting friend or associate so that he or she can show it to the people you know. The letter can be brief and businesslike, or longer and more informal.

Short Letter of Introduction

Dear Joan:

Sometime next month a colleague of mine, Jim Hausman, will be visiting Vail on his winter vacation.

He is single, pleasant, and a superb skier.

I've given him your telephone number, and suggested that he call you when he gets there. If you have time to meet him, I think you'll find him most enjoyable.

Sincerely,

Longer Letter of Introduction

This letter will introduce Howard Murphy, my colleague in the Music Department of Wayne State University.

Howard is doing a doctoral thesis on jazz musicians in Europe, and will be spending six months traveling on the Continent.

He is one of my most competent and imaginative students, and is an accomplished jazz musician in his own right.

He is especially interested in meeting both very young and very old European jazz musicians, and in discussing their contributions to the modern jazz idiom.

I have assured Howard that my European friends will respond as warmly and cordially to him as they always have to me.

And so, I shall be most appreciative of any professional or personal assistance you can offer.

Sincerely,

16. Club and Organization Correspondence

IF YOU BELONG to a club or organization, you may be responsible for writing and sending out announcements for meetings, fund-raising letters, and other kinds of correspondence. This chapter will give examples of different kinds of correspondence, and will offer suggestions about making it more interesting.

A WORD ABOUT POSTAGE: You may be able to reduce your postage expenses by applying to your post office for Third Class mailing privileges. Third Class rates for nonprofit organizations are about 75 percent less than First Class. And if you're not entitled to nonprofit status, you may get a commercial rate, which is still lower than First Class.

You'll have to pay an initial fee and an annual renewal fee for the Third Class permit. But if your mailing list is large enough, it may be well worth it.

REGULAR MEETING ANNOUNCEMENTS

Every meeting announcement should contain, as basic information, the name of the organization and the time, date, and place of the meeting.

A postal card is usually sufficient, and requires less of an investment in time and money than a letter.

The following is an example of a meeting announcement with the minimal amount of information on it, arranged as for a postal card:

Monthly Meeting
East Hampton Philatelic Society
Saturday, June 25
10:00 A.M.
At the home of Jim Tully
34 Anderson Avenue, Brookdale

Fred Maher, Secy.
Tel.: 123–4567

To attract the greatest possible number of members, you can do considerably more. It's usually helpful to say a few words about any special event that will take place at the meeting, as in the following announcement.

Teachers' Reading Group Meeting
Thursday, Sept. 14, 8 P.M.
Central Conference Room, Greer School
"HOW TO HANDLE THE HYPERACTIVE CHILD"
Billie Smith will present new information to
help you cope with this important problem.

74

BUSINESS MEETING ANNOUNCEMENTS

Many organizations devote one meeting a year to the conduct of special business. Here's a model for the kind of announcement that might be sent to members:

Notice of the 57th Annual Meeting
of the Joseph and Roberta David Charity Fund

The Annual Meeting of the Trustees of the Joseph and Roberta David Charity Fund will be held Sunday, June 1, 1980, at 3:00 P.M., at the home of Mr. and Mrs. Milton Freedberg, 1 Roundwood Road, Weston, Mass., for the purpose of considering and acting on the following matters:

1. Report of the Secretary
2. Report of the Treasurer
3. Report of the Advisory Committee on Disbursements
4. Distribution of Income
5. Election of Trustees
6. Such other business as may properly be brought before the meeting or any adjournment thereof.

Trustees are invited to bring their families.

Dora Agoos
Secretary

April 15, 1980

SPECIAL EVENTS ANNOUNCEMENTS

You may want to send out letters announcing a special event that your organization is sponsoring. Try to make the letter as exciting as possible. Here are some suggestions that will add zest:

1. Use colored paper instead of white.
2. Use white paper with a letterhead in colored ink.
3. Use paper larger than the usual eight-and-a-half by eleven inches.

The following letter will serve as a model for your own special events:

Dear Parents:

You're due for a tremendous pleasure in about six weeks.

That's when you'll be able to see "The Night Was Made for Music."

This delightful evening of music, dance and old-time vaudeville is being presented by the brilliant Stoddard High School Music Organization.

Some of the highlights you'll enjoy:

**Trick marching and playing by the
Prize-winning Fife & Drum Corps!

**Old-time group singing for the whole
audience! Led by Superintendent of
Schools Jim "Liberace" Mason

** Mini-Musical Comedy: A one-act,
singing/dancing/laugh-in guaranteed
to have you rolling in the aisles!

*** And More! More! More! ***

The evening will be fun—and more than fun: it will also be helping the Stoddard Athletic Scholarship Fund, which sends deserving students on to college.

Your contribution will be completely tax-deductible.

The happy event will take place on Friday evening, June 12, at 8:30, in the Stoddard High School Auditorium, Branch and Pine streets, Mapleville.

Tickets are $2.50 each. How many would you like?

Just fill in the coupon below, and send this letter back to us, along with your check or money order. We'll send your tickets immediately.

Or you can buy them at the school office, from 8:30 to 3:00 every weekday.

However you buy them, you'll be glad you did. It's going to be a memorable evening. Come! And have a grand time!

Cordially,

Freda Trowbridge
PTA Promotion Director

. . . .

Of course, I want to have a wonderful time! Send me_____tickets at once! I'm sending you $_____($2.50 per ticket) in this letter to cover the cost of them.

Name_____

Address_____

City_____ State_____ Zip_____

Did You Notice That:

1. *The first sentence talks about the enjoyable time the recipient will have.* This is much better than the more standard beginning, which runs along the lines of: "We announce a special event."

2. *The second paragraph identifies the event with an intriguing name.* A more traditional way of doing it is simply to call it a night of music. Similarly, any event can be dressed up by an interesting title. This makes it more attractive, because it sounds like something new and fresh.

3. *Some of the details are described in a colorful way.* If you're asking people to invest their time or money, tell them about what they're going to see in a way that will make them want to come.

4. *A reason why people should buy tickets is mentioned.* If the proceeds from the affair are going to a cause or fund, say so.

5. *Tax deductibility is important.* If you offer it, mention it.

6. *Note that the time, date, and place of the event are given near the end.* The reason is that this information would intrude at the beginning, which is devoted to an exciting description of the event.

7. *This letter has a coupon at the bottom as a money-saving way of getting a response.* The coupon might also be sent on a separate slip of paper.

8. *Adding a final encouragement is a good way to end the letter.*

9. *The signer of the letter should be clearly identified.* This is to remove any doubts in the recipient's mind about who's asking him to attend.

17. Spelling, Grammar and Clichés

EVEN PROFESSIONAL WRITERS make errors in spelling and grammar, and all but the most careful word craftsmen are guilty of committing clichés to paper.

It will be worth your while to read this chapter two or three times so that you will automatically avoid some of the more common errors.

FOGGY PHRASES

Each of the following lines begins with a foggy phrase—that is, a roundabout way of saying something that could be said much more succinctly. The words in parentheses are the ones to use in place of them.

In regard to (about, concerning)
In relation to (toward, to)
In connection with (of, in, on)
On the part of (for, among)
With reference to (on, about, concerning)
In view of (because, since)
In the event of (if)
In order to (to)
On behalf of (for)
In accordance with (with, by)
By means of (with, by)
In the case of (if, in)
In the matter of (in)
In the amount of (for)
For the purpose of (for)
In the majority of instances (usually)
In a number of cases (some)
On a few occasions (occasionally)
In the time of (during)

TIRED WORDS AND PHRASES

Here is a list of incorrect and aged phrases that should have been buried long ago. They are wrong, clumsy, wordy, or old-fashioned—or a combination of all four. Become familiar with them so that you can avoid them. This list, incidentally, is based on a similar list in *Plain Letters*, published by the General Services Administration.

At about "He will arrive at about nine o'clock." This is incorrect. Use "at" or "about" but not both.

Accompanied by The preposition *with* is usually better. "I am enclosing a form with this letter," not, "This letter is accompanied by a form."

Acquaint Use "tell" or "inform"; "acquaint" is both stiff and dated. "Advise" can also be replaced by "tell" or "inform."

Affect, effect "Affect" is a verb meaning *to modify or influence.* "Effect" may be a noun *or* a verb. As a verb, it means to accomplish or bring about; as a noun, it means outcome or result. Correct examples: "The accident affected our plans"; "The program has a good effect on my children"; "I think I can effect a change for the better."

All ready, already The first—all ready—is correctly used in the following example: "When the hour came, they were all ready." The second—already—is correctly used in the following example: "We have already written a letter." However, in this example, and in many other sentences, "already" is redundant and can be eliminated: "We have written a letter."

Alternative Avoid the phrase "the only other alternative." Instead, write: "the alternative."

Anxious is correct only when anxiety exists. If you really mean "eager," then use it.

Appreciate your informing me is clumsy. Try something simple, such as "please write me," or "please tell me."

Apt Often used incorrectly when the writer means "likely." Apt suggests a predisposition as: "A smart student is apt to get high marks." "Likely" suggests possibility, as: "A few bad apples are likely to spoil the barrel."

At all times "Always" is better.

At this time "Now" is better.

At the present time "Now" is better.

At an early date "Soon" is better.

At your earliest convenience "Soon" is usually better.

At the earliest possible moment "Soon" or "immediately" is better.

Attached please find
Attached herewith   "Attached" is enough;
Attached hereto   the other words are
unnecessary.

Between, among "Between" refers to only two; "among" to more than two.

Biannual means "twice a year." Semiannual means the same.

Biennial means "every two years."

Bimonthly means both "every two months" and "twice a month." Since its meaning is not immediately clear, avoid it and use alternatives such as "semi-monthly" for twice a month; and "every two months."

Commence "Begin" and "start" are less stiff and usually preferable.

Communicate, communication Avoid these long words if possible. Be specific: Instead of "communicate," say "write," "wire," or "telephone." Instead of "communication," say "letter," "telegram," or "memo."

Conclude Another stiff word. It's better to "end" or "close" a letter than to "conclude" it.

Continuously, continually The first word means "without interruption"; the second, "intermittently."

Demonstrates "Shows" is the simpler, preferable form.

Desire "If you wish" or "if you want" sounds better than "if you desire."

Determine is overworked. Use "decide" or "find out."

Different Often unnecessary; as in: We had six different choices for dinner.

Due to the fact that is a wordy way of saying "because."

Earliest practicable date "Practicable" is a hazy word; use "soon" or "immediately."

Effectuate "Effect" means the same thing and is shorter.

Enclosed herewith   "Enclosed" is enough

Enclosed please find   "Enclosed" is enough

Equivalent "Equal" is usually better and it is shorter.

Farther, further "Farther" implies distance; "further" implies quantity or degree. You walk farther; you hear nothing further.

Few, less "Few" implies numbers; "less" implies quantities: "Say fewer words, and speak less."

For your information Usually superfluous, and can be eliminated.

For the month of July Write: "for July"

For the reason that Write: "since," "because," or "as."

Fullest possible extent Say simply: "full extent" or "fully."

Furnish "Give" is shorter and more direct.

Implement "Carry out" is more direct.

In addition to Write: "besides."

In compliance with your request Write: "as you requested."

In a satisfactory manner Write: "satisfactorily"

In the near future Write: "soon."

In the event that Write: "if"

In the amount of Write: "for"

In the meantime Write: "meantime" or "meanwhile."

In order to Write: "to"

In regard to Write: "about"

In view of the fact that Write: "as"

Inasmuch as "As," "since," and "because" are much shorter.

Indicate "Show" is less overworked, shorter, and more direct.

Kindly Don't use it for "please." Write "Please reply," not "Kindly reply."

Liquidate How about "pay off," instead?

None as a subject is usually plural, unless a single subject is indicated. "None of the jobs are open." "None of the work is finished."

Notwithstanding the fact that A wordy way of saying "although" or "even though."

On Unnecessary in stating dates. "He arrived Monday," not "He arrived on Monday."

Previous to, prior to "Before" usually sounds better.

Principal, principle The noun "principal" means head or chief; it also means a capital sum. The adjective "principle" means "truth," "belief," "policy," "conviction," "general theory," or "rule."

Quite means "truly," "really," "wholly," or "positively." Avoid the phrases: "quite a few" and "quite some."

Rarely ever, seldom ever "Ever" is unnecessary.

Reside "Live" is preferable.

Submitted "Sent" is preferable and more direct.

Subsequent to "After" is shorter and more direct.

This is to inform you You can usually omit this phrase.

This is to thank you Can you use the shorter "Thank you"?

Utilize, utilization Use the shorter word "use."

Wish to apologize Say simple "I [or we] apologize."

Wish to advise Can usually be eliminated.

IMPROVING YOUR SPELLING

The following list contains words frequently misspelled. Learn them by heart and you'll avoid the most common errors. If you have a word about which you're doubtful, check it against this list or look it up in your dictionary.

absence	counsel	height	o'clock
accidentally	criticize	hero	omitted
accommodate	criticism	heroes	opinion
acknowledgment	deceive	heroine	opportunity
acquaint	decision	humorous	
acquaintance	definite		parallel
affect/effect	descend	image	parliament
aggravate	descend	imaginary	performance
all right	descendant	imagination	perhaps
altar/alter	describe	imagine	personal
altogether	description	immediately	personnel
amateur	desert	indispensable	pleasant
appearance	dessert	individual	possess
argument	develop	interest	precede
around	difference	interested	prejudice
athletic	different	irresponsible	president
attendance	disappear	its *(possessive)*	principal/principle
auxiliary	disappoint	it's *(contraction)*	probably
	dividend		proceed
bargain	doesn't (contraction)	jealous	professor
beginning	don't (contraction)	judgment	promissory
behavior	during	judicious	pronunciation
believe	effect/affect	kernel	prophecy
beneficial	eighth	knead	prophesy
benefited	embarrass	know-how	purchasable
benefiting	environment	knowledgeable	quiet
bicentennial	equipment		quite
bouyant	equipped	laboratory	
business	escape	leisure	receive
	exaggerate	license	recommend
career	excellent	literature	referred
catalog	excited	lonely	regrettable
cemetery	excitement	loose	relieve
certain	exciting	lose	responsibility
changeable	exercise	losing	restaurant
character	existence		rhythm
chief	experience	maintenance	
choose	experiment	marriage	salable
chosen		marries	schedule
commit	familiar	meant	seize
commitment	fascinate	mischievous	sense
committed	February	monetary	separate
committee	finally	municipal	similar
committing	foreign		simplify
competition	foreigners	necessary	society
complete	forth	necessity	speech
comptroller	forty	ninety	stationary/stationery
conscientious	friend	ninth	stopped
conscious		noticeable	stopping
consensus	glamorous	obstacle	strength
convenience	glamour	occasion	studied
coolly	government	occasionally	studies
council	grammar	occurrence	study
	grievance	occurred	studying

success	thousandth	ultimately	woman/women
successful	together	unmistakable	writer
superintendent	to/too	until	writing
supersede	tragedy		written
surprise	transferred	villain	
	transient		yield
technicality	tried	Wednesday	you're *(contraction)*
tendency	tries	weird	your
their/there	truly	whether	

SOME SUGGESTIONS FOR IMPROVING YOUR SPELLING

If you're serious about improving your spelling, you would be wise to invest in one or more of the good, inexpensive paperback books on the subject.

Among them are: *Correct Spelling Made Easy,* by Norman Lewis, Dell Publishing Co.; *Spelling Your Way to Success,* by Joseph Mersand and Francis Griffith, Barron's Educational Series, Inc.; *Spell It Right!* by Harry Shaw, Barnes & Noble Books; *6 Minutes a Day to Perfect Spelling* by Harry Shefter, Pocket Books; *Words at Work,* by Joseph Bellafiore, Amsco School Publications, Inc.

Several suggestions will help you to improve your spelling almost immediately:

1. *Use your body muscles to spell.* When you have trouble spelling a word correctly, trace the letters on a sheet of paper with your index finger. Do this several times. You may find that your muscles "memorize" the letters. This works very well for some people, not so well for others.

2. *Draw a picture with the letters.* If you're at all artistic, you may find it very useful to arrange the letters so that they form a picture, as for example, in this illustration of the word MARRY. (One "R" is backward which should trigger your memory to recall the correct spelling.)

The picture need not even look like the word. All that's necessary is that you remember the picture. If you can remember it, you'll be able to recall the parts that went into it, and you may be able to spell the word properly.

3. *Associate the word with a clear mental picture.* If you find yourself repeatedly misspelling a word, you may find it helpful to create a mental picture that will remind you of the correct spelling. Here are two examples:

Cemetery. People frequently spell it incorrectly. Suppose this is your problem. You might want to teach yourself to remember that the correct order of the letters in the middle of the word is "m-e-t-e."

Let your mind wander to a familiar word that contains those letters—for example, "meter." Then create a picture in your mind of a cemetery whose headstones have parking meters on them.

From now on, whenever you think of the word "cemetery," you will think of parking meters, and you'll remember that the word is spelled with three e's.

While this process is complicated to describe, it can be done in a few seconds, once you have the idea. Here's another example:

Principal/principle. Many people have trouble remembering how to spell these words correctly. Applying our technique, we know that a "principle" is a rule, and that both "principle" and "rule" end in "le." In your mind, picture a large, official-looking parchment scroll with the word "rule" written on it. From now on, whenever you have to write the word "principle," you'll remember that scroll—and if the word you want means "rule," you'll immediately know the correct spelling.

4. To solve the common problem of deciding whether "i" or "e" comes first in such words as "receive" and "relieve," here's the complete version of the old, helpful rhyme:

> Put i before e
> Except after c,
> Or when sounded like *a*
> As in *neighbor* and *weigh*,
> And except *seize* and *seizure*,
> And also *leisure*,
> *Weird, height,* and *either,*
> *Forfeit* and *neither.*

In addition to these four techniques, there are several others most experts recommend. All of them require practice—there's no easy way to become proficient.

1. *Pronounce the word carefully and correctly.* "Allusion" and "illusion" sound similar when carelessly pronounced, and are often confused in the spelling. "Color" and "collar," "carton" and "cartoon," "gesture" and "jester" are all words that almost sound alike. But if you pronounce them carefully, you'll reduce your chances of misspelling them.

2. *Try to create a picture of the word in your mind.* If you can create such a picture, you'll often be able to summon it when you want to spell the word. Here's how some specialists recommend creating a picture:

First, pronounce the word carefully. Check the pronunciation in a dictionary if you're not sure.

Second, if the word has one syllable, study each letter in it. If it has more than one syllable, study each syllable in turn, and say it over to yourself.

Third, close your eyes. Now, if it's a one-syllable word, say it out loud and spell it out. If it has more than one syllable, say each syllable out loud and spell it out.

Fourth, open your eyes and make sure you've spelled the word correctly.

Do this at least four or five times: Look at the word, close your eyes and spell it, then open your eyes to check it. Before long, you'll have a picture of the word in your mind.

3. *Use a dictionary.* When you're not certain of the spelling of a word, run for the dictionary as you would run for a glass of water if you were dying of thirst. The wonderful thing about a dictionary is that *it has the answers.* Dictionaries are certain, direct, brief, and delighted to tell you what they know. Use one. Obviously, it takes more time than guessing, especially if you don't know the correct spelling of the beginning of the word. But the dictionary habit will repay you.

It is essential that you get a good hardcover dictionary, although a number of satisfactory paperbook editions are available. The *American College Dictionary, Webster's New Collegiate Dictionary, Webster's New World Dictionary,* and the *Thorndike-Barnhart Comprehensive Desk Dictionary* are standard, high-quality works. The *American Heritage Dictionary of the English Language, Webster's New International Dictionary, Funk and Wagnall's New Standard Dictionary,* and the two-volume *The Shorter Oxford Dictionary* are larger dictionaries. Incidentally, before buying a dictionary, you should know that any publisher can use the name "Webster's." Consequently, a number of low-quality dictionaries bear the name. World Publishing and G. & C. Merriam are two publishers of high-quality Webster's dictionaries.

18. Stationery and Letterheads

JUST AS CLOTHING gives an impression about the wearer, stationery gives an impression about the writer. Attractive stationery and letterheads give a good impression of the writer; poor-quality stationery and letterheads give an opposite impression.

Your local stationery store or the stationery department of a department store will have sample books of different kinds and sizes of stationery, both paper and cards. You'll find stationery available in an endless range of styles and colors. The stationery you use for your purely personal correspondence is a personal matter. But when you're writing any other kind of letter, you might want to consider these suggestions.

Paper comes in different weights. Generally, the heavier the weight, the better the feel of the paper in the hand. If you ask for twenty-pound rag bond paper, you'll get a good-quality paper with a good feel to it.

Paper measuring eight and a half by eleven inches is standard for most business and professional correspondence. You can buy small packages of it at five-and-ten-cent stores. Or, you can buy it from stationery stores in packages of five hundred—called reams. This is usually the least expensive way to buy plain paper.

You may, of course, want a smaller size—seven and a half by ten and a half is common, and is a good size if you write short letters.

Smaller sizes have become popular in recent years, especially for brief notes. Also quite common are sheets that are folded in half.

When we speak of sheets, we must include everything from paper to heavy card stock. For social correspondence, no one size is more appropriate than another. One rule of thumb may be helpful: The longer the message, the larger the stationery can be.

You can also buy "erasable" paper—paper that is treated so that typewritten errors may be cleanly erased. The finished letter usually looks very professional because there is virtually no trace of errors. Be careful not to rub this paper unintentionally, however, because the ink smudges far more easily than on regular paper. For this reason, you should never use erasable paper for a manuscript because it may be handled a great deal by many people, and the typed copy smudges from the shuffling.

Social stationery is available in a rainbow of colors and many patterns. Traditionally, women have used tinted stationery and men have confined themselves to white or off-white. But this, too, has been changing, and men's stationery in bold colors has become both acceptable and fashionable.

MONOGRAMS AND LETTERHEADS

Monograms and letterheads do dress up stationery. If you plan to use your stationery mainly for personal correspondence, monogrammed stationery will be perfectly suitable. But if you plan to use it also for correspondence with strangers, you might want to consider paper that carries your name, address, and telephone number.

When you visit a stationery department to select paper, you'll find a variety of monograms and letterhead styles to choose from. It is also possible to have an original designed. To do this, your best bet is to talk to a professional illustrator. Your stationery store may be able to supply you with some names, or you can check the Yellow Pages of the telephone book under "Artists."

KINDS OF PRINTING

Of the four kinds of printing usually available, the most expensive is engraving. An engraved letterhead or monogram is carved on a block of metal. On the printed stationery, the letters are actually raised above the rest of the paper, creating a very luxurious appearance. Once the engraved plate is made, it can be reused, so the initial cost comes down considerably on reorders.

A second kind of printing simulates engraving by means of a very thick ink which you can feel when you run your finger over the printing. This so-called raised or electrostatic printing looks good and is reasonably priced. Incidentally, raised printing can be made to look shiny or dull. Tell the printer your preference.

A third kind of printing is letterpress. In letterpress, the printing is done by metal letters which create a good, sharp impression.

A fourth kind of printing is called offset—the printing is done by a metal plate onto which your letterhead has been photographically transferred. This style is usually the least expensive; the quality and appearance are generally not quite as sharp as with letterpress.

A WORD ABOUT ENVELOPES

If you're buying special stationery, buy matching envelopes; your letters will look better. For a really luxurious touch, you might want to see what's available in lined envelopes—envelopes that have a paper lining glued inside. These combinations are expensive, but they usually look lovely.

FOLDING UP

The fewer the number of folds in your stationery, the better it will look when it comes out of the envelope. So here are some suggestions for minimizing the number of folds.

Start with paper that is slightly smaller than the width of the envelope.

Then, see if it will fit into the envelope with just one fold across the middle.

If it won't fit with one fold across the middle, fold it into three equal sections—which is the way most business letters are folded.

If that still doesn't do the trick, fold the letter in half from top to bottom, and then fold it horizontally in half or in thirds.

PEN, PENCIL, AND TYPEWRITER

If you're over six years old, never use a pencil to write a letter, unless you don't care what kind of an impression you're making. A letter written in pencil looks childish and amateurish.

Most social correspondence is still written by hand, because it looks more personal than typewritten letters. If you're writing a business letter and can type reasonably neatly, use a typewriter. A typewritten letter looks as if it means business, and in most cases, your letter will be taken more seriously.

LETTERHEAD SAMPLES

The varieties of attractive letterhead styles are endless. These samples can merely suggest some of them. And, seeing and touching the handsome papers available is one of the more civilized joys of this world. A stylish letterhead and stationery can do wonders for your soul and your public image. It's worth investing both time and money to get exactly what you want.

Papers by Crane

Mrs. Alfred G. Bellows
445 Lucemont Terrace
Seattle, Washington 98116

RANDOLPH P. JENNERS
4250 PARK AVENUE
NEW YORK, NEW YORK 10016

harvey
& tracy
associates, inc.

Page, Arbitrio & Resen

Designers
595 Madison Avenue
New York, New York 10022
212–421–8190

Mrs. Stephen T. Waltham
428 LOWELL DRIVE
MINNEAPOLIS, MINNESOTA 55409

rsa
RON STRASNER ASSOCIATES

8743 SUNSET BOULEVARD / LOS ANGELES, CALIFORNIA 90069 / (213) 659-0308

WILLIAM B. LAWSON

RICHARD D. BOND
420 CRANDALL TERRACE
SAN FRANCISCO, CALIFORNIA 94112

19. Important Postal Information

THE UNITED STATES Postal Service provides many special services. Here's a run-down on some of the more important ones. If you'd like more information about any of these, or about other services, consult your local post office.

CLASSES OF MAIL

First Class mail. Handwritten or typewritten matter, bills, and statements of account are sent First Class. The Postal Service often sends First Class mail weighing under 12 ounces Airmail. Maximum weight for First Class mail is 70 pounds; maximum size, 100 inches in length and girth combined. If your mailing isn't letter size, mark it "First Class" on all sides so that it will receive first-class handling.

Second Class mail. Generally used by newspaper and periodical publishers.

Third Class mail. Used most often for large mailings of printed materials and parcels weighing under a pound. There are a number of categories of Third Class mail, and these are best explained by your postmaster.

Fourth Class mail (Parcel Post). For sending packages. Your post office has information on special rates for books, records, material for the blind, catalogs, and international mailing.

FOR FAST DELIVERY

Airmail. Can weigh up to 70 pounds and have a maximum size of 100 inches in length and girth combined. Mark the package or envelope "Airmail," clearly, in large letters, so postal employees will give it priority handling.

Aerogramme. Special prestamped stationery for international correspondence. Folds into a self-enclosed envelope; available at all post offices.

Express mail. Guarantees overnight delivery for letters and parcels. Available only in certain cities, so check with your postmaster.

Special Delivery. Special Delivery mail is given prompt delivery at the destination post office in areas served by city carriers and within a one-mile radius of any post office. Special Delivery is provided on rural and star routes.

Mailgram. A combination of letter and telegram. You phone or deliver your message to your local Western Union office, which telegraphs it anywhere in the United States. The postman delivers it the next day. Check your post office for rates.

MAILING VALUABLES

Insured mail. Insurance up to $200 is available for Third and Fourth Class mail, and Air Parcel Post. Irreplaceable articles, regardless of value, and all items worth more than $200, should be sent by Registered Mail.

Registered Mail. The safest way to send valuables. Gives you insurance protection up to $10,000 for domestic mail. For an additional fee, you can get a return receipt showing to whom, when, and where the mail was delivered.

C.O.D. mail. Collect-on-Delivery service may be used when the addressee has ordered merchandise. Upon delivery of the package, the addressee pays the amount due the mailer for the merchandise and postage, plus the money-order fee.

Money Orders. Money orders are a safe way to send money through the mail and may be purchased at all post offices. If your money order is lost or stolen, it will be replaced. International money orders may also be purchased at first class post offices.

Obtaining Proof of Mailing

Certificate of Mailing. If you want proof that you've mailed something, you can buy a Certificate of Mailing for a nominal fee. It provides no insurance coverage, nor does the post office keep any record.

Certified Mail. You get a mailing receipt and a record of delivery is made at the addressee's post office. Certified Mail travels no faster than First Class, and offers no extra security or payment for loss. For security, use Registered Mail.

Return Receipts. The Return Receipt is your proof of delivery. It's available on insured mail of more than $15 value, and on Certified and Registered Mail. The Return Receipt tells who signed for the item and the date it was delivered. For additional fees, you can either obtain a receipt showing the exact address of delivery, or you can restrict delivery of your mail to the addressee only (state and federal officials excluded).

20. Formats for Letters

Good-looking letters make the reader want to look at them; bad-looking letters tend to discourage readership. The model letter below follows a standard format. The paragraphs following the letter discuss the format.

①

Richard C. Struthers
1234 Caraway Boulevard ⑧
Hazeltine, Mo. 12345
(987) 654—3210

March 15, 1975 ②

Account No. 421—239A ⑩

Mr. Victor H. Drungo ③
Executive Vice-President
Forsberg's Department Store
112 Columbus Avenue
Denver, Colo. 45678
④
Dear Mr. Drungo:
   I'm enclosing a check for $19, which will bring my account with your store up ⑤
to date.
   Please send me a written confirmation that you've received this payment, and
that there is no balance due.
   In the future, when a similar problem arises, I'd be most appreciative if you:
   a. Let me know before such a long period has passed.
   b. Send me an itemized statement.
   I'm glad that we were finally able to straighten out this problem, and I trust that
we'll avoid similar situations in the future. ⑨
                  Sincerely, ⑥

           Wilma Anderson Struthers ⑦

1. *Leaving a generous margin on both sides, and at the top and bottom, will give your letter a good-looking "frame."* Margins of less than one and a half inches make the page look crowded and unattractive.

2. *Remember to write in the date.* This is especially important in business letters, when you may need to refer to the correspondence at a later time.

3. *If the letter is very short, you may want to double-space it in order to fill up the page.* Otherwise, single-spacing is preferable.

4. *There should be a double space between the recipient's address and the salutation.* Some people also double-space between paragraphs, and do not indent the first

line of the paragraph. Others like to double-space and indent. Still others prefer to indent but not to double-space. All are acceptable.

5. *Keeping your sentences and paragraphs short increases the readability of your letter.* As a general rule, try to keep each paragraph under four sentences. And try to keep each sentence under three lines. (Notice how your daily newspaper does it: paragraphs are frequently no more than one sentence long.)

6. *Some people prefer to put the complimentary closing just to the right of the center, as here.* On typed letters, others prefer it flush against the left margin. Again, it's a matter of personal preference: both are acceptable now, although the version shown here is more traditional.

7. *On a typed letter, if the signature is the same as the name on the letterhead, there's no need to type the name under the signature.* If the signature is different from the name on the letterhead, it's a good idea to type the signature name under the written signature.

8. *If you are writing on paper with no letterhead, it's customary to write your address at the top of the page on the right side.*

9. *On a typed letter, you'll normally double-space between:* the date and the recipient's name and address; the recipient's name and address and the salutation; the last line of the last paragraph and the complimentary closing.

10. *Place important identifying numbers at the top of the page.* This makes it easier for the recipient to find your file quickly.

21. Correct Forms of Address

In the following tables, where the term "Mr." is used, it should be understood that if the official is a woman, she should be addressed as Ms., Miss, Mrs., or Madam. Be sure to include the correct Zip Code number in your address.

U.S. Government Officials

Person	Address	Salutation
The President	The President The White House Washington, D.C. 20510	Dear Mr. President:
The Vice President	The Vice-President United States Senate Washington, D.C. 20510	Dear Mr. Vice-President:
Chief Justice of the United States	The Chief Justice of the United States The Supreme Court Washington, D.C. 20543	Dear Mr. Chief Justice:
Associate Justice	Mr. Justice Jones The Supreme Court Washington, D.C. 20543	Dear Mr. Justice:
U.S. Senator	The Honorable John Jones United States Senate Washington, D.C. 20510	Dear Senator Jones:
U.S. Representative	The Honorable John Jones The United States House of Representatives Washington, D.C.	Dear Mr. Jones:
Speaker of the House of Representatives	The Honorable John Jones Speaker of the House of Representatives Washington, D.C.	Dear Mr. Speaker:
All other U.S. Government Civilian Officials	Mr. John Jones Title	Dear Mr. Jones:

Person	Address	Salutation

State and Local Officials

Person	Address	Salutation
Governor	The Honorable John Jones Governor of (State)	Dear Governor Jones:
Lieutenant Governor	The Honorable John Jones Lt. Governor of (State)	Dear Mr. Jones:
State Senator	The Honorable John Jones The State Senate State Capitol	Dear Senator Jones:
State Assemblyman or Representative	The Honorable John Jones House of Representatives (or The Assembly) State Capitol	Dear Mr. Jones:

Court Officials

Person	Address	Salutation
Federal Judge	The Honorable John Jones United States District Judge	Dear Judge Jones:
State or Local Judge	The Honorable John Jones Judge of the Children's Court	Dear Judge Jones:

U.S. Diplomatic Officials

Person	Address	Salutation
U.S. Ambassador	The Honorable John Jones American Ambassador	Dear Mr. Ambassador:
U.S. Consul-General, Consul, Vice-Consul or Chargé d'Affaires or	John Jones, Esq. American Consul General American Consul or American Vice-Consul or American Chargé d'Affaires	Dear Sir:
U.S. Delegate to the United Nations	Mr. John Jones Chief of the United States Mission to the United Nations	Dear Mr. Jones:

Foreign Officials

Person	Address	Salutation
Ambassador to the U.S.	His Excellency John Jones Ambassador of (Country) (Always use the full name of the ambassador's country except for British officials, who should be addressed as British Ambassador, British Minister, etc.)	Dear Mr. Ambassador:

Person	Address	Salutation
Foreign Minister	The Honorable John Jones	Dear Mr. Minister:
Diplomatic Official with a Personal Title	His Excellency, Count John Jones Ambassador of (Country)	Dear Mr. Ambassador:
Secretary-General of the United Nations	His Excellency John Jones Secretary-General of the United Nations	Dear Mr. Jones:
President of a Republic	His Excellency John Jones President of the Republic of (Country)	Dear Mr. President:
Prime Minister of Great Britain	The Right Honorable John Jones, M.P. Prime Minister	My dear Mr. Prime Minister:
Prime Minister of Canada	The Right Honorable John Jones, C.M.C. Prime Minister of the Dominion of Canada	My dear Mr. Jones:

Members of the Armed Forces

The formula for addressing most Army, Navy, Coast Guard and Marine officers and enlisted men is: Full rank plus full name plus comma plus abbreviation of branch of service. The abbreviations of the branches of service are: Army—U.S.A.; Army Reserve—U.S.A.R.; Navy—U.S.N.; Naval Reserve—U.S.N.R.; Coast Guard—U.S.C.G.; Coast Guard Reserve—U.S.C.G.R.; Marine Corps—U.S.M.C.; Marine Corps Reserve—U.S.M.C.R. When the addressee is retired, put (Ret.) after the service initials.

Thus, the correct address for a retired brigadier general in the Army Reserve would be:

Brigadier General John Jones, U.S.A.R. (Ret.)

In the following table, the dash after the full name stands for the correct branch of service.

General	General John Jones, —	Dear General Jones:
Lieutenant General	Lieutenant General John Jones, —	Dear General Jones:
Major General	Major General John Jones, —	Dear General Jones:
Brigadier General	Brigadier General John Jones, —	Dear General Jones:
Colonel	Colonel John Jones, —	Dear Colonel Jones:
Lieutenant Colonel	Lieutenant Colonel John Jones, —	Dear Colonel Jones:
Major	Major John Jones, —	Dear Major Jones:
Captain	Captain John Jones, —	Dear Captain Jones:
First Lieutenant	First Lieutenant John Jones, —	Dear Lieutenant Jones:

Person	Address	Salutation
Second Lieutenant	Second Lieutenant John Jones, —	Dear Lieutenant Jones:
Army Chaplain	Chaplain John Jones (Rank), —	Dear Chaplain:
Fleet Admiral	Fleet Admiral John Jones, —	Dear Admiral Jones:
Vice Admiral	Vice Admiral John Jones, —	Dear Admiral Jones:
Rear Admiral	Rear Admiral John Jones, —	Dear Admiral Jones:
Commander	Commander John Jones, —	Dear Commander Jones:
Lieutenant Commander	Lieutenant Commander John Jones, —	Dear Commander Jones:
Lieutenant	Lieutenant John Jones, —	Dear Lieutenant Jones:
Lieutenant, Junior Grade	Lieutenant, J.G. John Jones, —	Dear Lieutenant Jones:
Ensign	Ensign John Jones, —	Dear Mr. Jones:
Navy Chaplain	(Rank and full name, followed by (Ch.C) and service branch, e.g., Captain John Jones (Ch.C) U.S.N.	Dear Chaplain:
Airman	Airman John Jones, —	Dear Airman Jones:
Corporal	Corporal John Jones,—	Dear Corporal Jones:
Master Sergeant	Master Sergeant John Jones, —	Dear Sergeant Jones:
Midshipman	Midshipman John Jones United States Naval Academy	Dear Midshipman Jones:
Petty Officers	(Full rank plus full name plus comma plus branch of service)	Dear Mr. Jones:
Private	(Same as above)	Dear Private Jones:
Seaman	(Same as above)	Dear Seaman Jones:
Specialist	(Same as above)	Dear Specialist Jones:
Warrant Officer	(Same as above)	Dear Mr. Jones:

Catholic Clergy

Person	Address	Salutation
The Pope	His Holiness The Pope Vatican City Italy	Your Holiness:
Cardinal	His Eminence John Cardinal Jones Archbishop of (Area)	Dear Cardinal Jones:
Archbishop	The Most Reverend John Jones Archbishop of (Area)	Dear Archbishop:
Bishop	The Most Reverend John Jones Bishop of (Area)	Dear Bishop:
Abbot	The Right Reverend John Jones Abbot of (Abbey)	Dear Father Abbot:
Canon	The Very Reverend Canon John Jones Canon of (Church)	Dear Canon Jones:

Person	Address	Salutation
Monsignor	The Right (or Very)* Reverend Msgr. John Jones	Dear Monsignor Jones:
Brother	Brother John Jones	Dear Brother Jones:
Superior of a Brotherhood and Priest	The Very Reverend John Jones (Title)	Dear Father Superior:
Priest	The Reverend John Jones	Dear Father Jones:
Sister Superior	The Reverend Sister Superior	Dear Sister Superior:
Sister	Sister (Full religious name)	Dear Sister:
Mother Superior of Sisterhood	The Reverend Mother Superior (Name of Convent)	Dear Reverend Mother:
Member of Community	Mother (Full name) (Name of Convent)	Dear Mother (Last name):

Protestant Clergy

Anglican Archbishop	To His Grace The Lord Archbishop of (Area)	Dear Archbishop:
Presiding Bishop of The Protestant Episcopal Church in the U.S.	The Most Reverend John Jones Presiding Bishop of the Protestant Episcopal Church in America	Dear Bishop:
Protestant Episcopal Bishop	The Right Reverend James Jones Bishop of (Area)	Dear Bishop:
Protestant Archdeacon	The Venerable John Jones The Archdeacon of (Area) Diocese of (Area)	Dear Archdeacon:
Dean	The Very Reverend John Jones Dean of (Cathedral or Seminary)	Dear Dean Jones:
Protestant Minister or Priest	The Reverend John Jones	Dear Mr. Jones: (If minister has a doctoral degree, e.g., Ph.D., D.D., may be addressed, "Dear Dr. Jones:"

Jewish Clergy

Rabbi	Rabbi John Jones	Dear Rabbi Jones: (If Rabbi has a doctoral degree, e.g., Ph.D., D.D., may be addressed, "Dear Dr. Jones:")

*Depends on rank or other titles. If in doubt, consult Official Catholic Directory.

Index